SURVIVING SOCCER

SURVIVING SOCCER

A Chill Parent's Guide
to Carpools,
Calendars,
Coaches, Clubs,
and Corner Kicks

KAREN SCHOLL

Copyright © 2025 by Karen Scholl

No part of this publication may be reproduced, stored in a retrieval system, or transmitted in any form by any means, electronic, mechanical, photocopying, or otherwise, without the prior written permission of the publisher, Triumph Books LLC, 814 North Franklin Street, Chicago, Illinois 60610.

Library of Congress Cataloging-in-Publication Data available upon request.

This book is available in quantity at special discounts for your group or organization. For further information, contact:

Triumph Books LLC
814 North Franklin Street
Chicago, Illinois 60610
(312) 337-0747
www.triumphbooks.com

Printed in China
ISBN: 978-1-63727-789-8
Editorial production and design by Alex Lubertozzi

To Noah and Max,
I loved to watch you play.

Contents

Introduction 1

Part I: Get in Position

1. Programs 7
2. Tryouts. 19
3. Parent Roles. 31

Part II: Get to Practice

4. Schedules + Punctuality 51
5. Cars + Parking Lots 57
6. Driving + Carpools. 67

Part III: Get Your Game On

7. Packing + Planning 83
8. Sideline Strategy. 101
9. Injuries. 117
10. Cheering. 129
11. It All Started So Innocently 139

Acknowledgments 145

Introduction

If you think signing your kid up for soccer will check a lot of the boxes good parents like you worry about, you're not wrong. Fresh air and exercise? Check. A team full of ready-made friends? Yep. Multiple hours a week when your kid will be on a field, not a device? You bet. And then there are all those life lessons: teamwork, time management, resilience, respect. Seems a lot easier than getting them the puppy they've been begging for, right? Plus, there's always that 2 percent chance your kid will get a college scholarship. (Besides, over Fido's lifetime, you would spend enough on him to cover a couple semesters of in-state tuition.)

Maybe you've even imagined how signing your kid up for soccer could change your own life. All that free time you'll have while they're at practice. Gorgeous Saturday afternoons cheering on the sidelines. Family bonding during car rides and weekend tournaments. New parent-friends you are literally scheduled to hang out with several times a week. Surely they'll become your besties, right?

That's the dream, for sure. But after 16 years of soccer-parenting two kids, I can tell you that's not the reality. Not quite.

Yes, soccer is a beautiful game. But it can also be a test—of your stamina, your wit, and your sideline savvy. Do you have what it takes to survive soccer? The following quiz is just a preview ➤

- Can you conquer rush-hour traffic to get your kid to practice two to five days a week—between guitar lessons, Hebrew School, and doctor/orthodontist/allergy appointments?
- Can you locate their left shin guard, inhaler, and lucky headband in the 30 seconds remaining until you have to be in the car so your kid is not late?
- Can you keep your cool when the team admin texts that tonight's game got moved up an hour?
- Can you defrost yet another prepackaged meal for dinner knowing that most of your family members won't have time to eat it, and the one who will is going to refuse because it's gross?
- Can you de-escalate your response when you get to work and find the important science worksheet that was due today in your backseat?
- Can you defeat your spouse in a rock-paper-scissors battle over which one of you has to enforce bath time with your kid at 10:00 PM on a school night?
- Can you rein in your reaction while the growing number of trophies, plaques, and medals

that your kid insists you display in the living room transform your décor from minimalist chic to discount sports shop?

- Can you stomach spending all the free time you don't have with a group of people you barely know? (And one or two you can barely stand?)
- Can you handle the looks from the parents chatting in the parking lot during practice while you log in to an all-staff video call in your car?
- Can you resist shaming the mom of the new kid for the unsanctioned, high-fructose snacks she broke out at halftime, just in case she's a viable carpool partner?
- Can you let your kid accept a ride with Cameron's dad, who always talks about politics and religion and totally thinks your kid should come to one of their church lock-ins?
- Can you drum up clever carpool conversations while avoiding subjects including school, homework, friends, the news, Kaylee's haircut, and the sleepover that only half the kids were invited to?
- Can you calculate whether it's too late in the season to ask Ryan's mom, who you sit by and talk to at every game, what her name is?
- Can you live with knowing that your most beautiful and embarrassing parenting moments will be witnessed by dozens of families you either like or dislike so much that you

would rather stand naked in front of them and read your diary out loud?

Think you can survive? Fill up your water bottle, buckle your seatbelt, and pay close attention.

PART I

GET IN POSITION

CHAPTER 1

Programs

Welcome to the world of youth soccer. Leave your ego at the door.

So your kid wants to play soccer. If you're done replacing broken lamps, fixing ball-shaped dents in your walls, and coaxing your pets back out from under your bed, it's time to find your kid a soccer team.

Don't start Googling or Facebook-stalking leagues and coaches just yet. First you need to understand the two-headed beast that is youth soccer. Noggin No. 1 is rec. Friendly. Approachable. Easy-peasy. And then there's club, rec's I-might-be-too-cool-for-you fraternal twin.

To the untrained eye, recreational and club leagues look a lot alike. Both get your kid on a team with a uniform, basic equipment, and a schedule of games. But one will bankrupt you and get you out of large family gatherings, while the other will have you rethinking your life choices.

7 REASONS YOUR FRIENDS WILL JUDGE YOU FOR LETTING YOUR KID PLAY SPORTS

I want you to hear this from me, because pretty soon you're going to hear it from people who know you well enough to stop you in the grocery store and talk about the weather while they judge you for what's in your cart.

As a seasoned parent, by now you're pretty used to other parents' jealousy—the uncomfortable smiles and over-the-top platitudes you got each time your kid won the science fair, wore the coolest Halloween costume, or sold the most raffle tickets.

But sports envy is next level. As soon as you start adding your kid's soccer highlights to your feed—and we've all done it—you'll quickly find out what your social media friends think about your parenting skills.

The shift from fake compliments to blatant hostility is swift. Keep a watch on some of your favorite posts, like, "Another championship in the books!" or, "Poor Liam played the entire game and didn't get a single break!" or, "So generous of the club to fly our family to Disney so Logan could play a tournament with the academy team!" The comments will start reading like a *60 Minutes* expose on the dark underbelly of the $37.5 billion youth sports industry. The premise of their arguments? Organized sports ruin children. The truth? Kids love trophies. We all do.

Regardless, you need to be ready when they come after your parenting credentials. In true social media fashion, these attacks will be launched not with old-fashioned insults, but sharply worded grudges and stories about their sister's neighbor's coworker's son who was cut from his soccer team and turned to a life of video games and barbecue pork rinds.

1 "Losing isn't healthy for kids." —@MyKidsAreAllWinners
What this kind-hearted mom means is, if you really love your children, the way she loves hers, you'll protect them for as long as you can from everything that could get in the way of their happiness. What she's actually saying is that her kids lack fundamental coping skills, and that the promise of ice cream with sprinkles is her most powerful parenting tool. Let's check back with her in 10 years and see exactly what her kids are winning.

SURVIVING SOCCER

2 **"Winning creates too much pressure."**
—*@ThatGuyInAccounting*
You spend enough time with him at the office to know there's a reason he's been passed over for a promotion three times. He thinks you're pushing your kid in over their head and setting a bad example for how children should spend their time. His skepticism of "the system" and distrust for authority play out in his social media feed alongside regular posts about how his favorite professional sports team really needs to fire the coach, rethink their strategy, or dump their MVP if they want a chance at the playoffs. No wonder he doesn't have time to do any work.

3 **"Rules rob kids of their innate creativity and spontaneity."**
—*@FreeRangeFam*
More of a caption-less-photo sort of family, their feed is full of candid grayscale pictures. From every one of their nine home births to the chaos of their everyday life, each snapshot reveals a little more detail than you ever wanted to see. (Hard pass on the placenta pics, thanks.) The hearts and likes they've given your posts over the years demonstrate how deeply they care about you, which is why they just want to make sure you're not cheating your kid out of an authentic life.

4 **"Coaches are on power trips and just like bossing kids around."**
—*@BecauseISaidSo*
Truth be told, you're not sure why you're still friends with this former soccer dad. He pulled his kid off your team midway through the season when you both had seven-year-olds. The games were actually a lot more pleasant without him yelling at his son and criticizing the coach. While you haven't seen this dad in person in years, his staunch anti-school-levy stance and his posts about the ludicrous lessons his kids get from their overpaid teachers are a growing presence on your feed even though he disables comments on all his posts.

Programs

5 **"When parents don't prioritize family time, kids pay the price."**
—*@WorldsBestMom*
With photos of loving siblings, made-from-scratch dinners, family movie night, family game night, family craft night, family chore night, and quotes from all the parenting books that she and her husband read out loud to each other after the kids go to bed, her feed is a testimony that if you act more like a camp counselor than a chauffeur, your kids will be better off. She doesn't need to prove that she knows what she's talking about, the mug her kids gave her says so.

6 **"An organized sport is too big of a commitment for a child."**
—*@MotheringIsNotSmothering*
Sometimes it takes an outsider to show you what's really going on in your life, and this mom is selfless like that. She's just trying to help you see that a 90-minute practice three days a week and the opportunity for a kid to get fresh air and forget about things like a rough math test or an embarrassing lunch-table gaffe, may not be right at this age. As long as she's hovering over her kids, she may as well check on everyone else's.

7 **"Your kid is ruining sports for other kids."**
—*@AfraidOfBeingOrdinary*
In so many ways, we're all just trying to protect our kids. This friend from your then-toddler's Mommy & Me group is merely trying to make sure you don't take any opportunities away from her little bookworm as they grow up. If you let your kid play soccer three or four days a week, their skills are likely to improve. If her kid goes outside someday, they won't be able to kick the ball as far as your kid will. How is that fair?

SURVIVING SOCCER

Pick the Right Team for Your Kid

Whether they start soccer when they're four or 14, most kids begin on a rec team. But the question you need to ask yourself is, should they stay there? Is the recreational curriculum, which is a combination of third grade recess soccer and the TikTok videos of two-year-old soccer savants, still meeting your kid's needs?

Maybe your kid wants more. Maybe they asked for a drum set because if they can't play more soccer, then it's the only other thing in the whole entire world that they want to do. Maybe your therapist told you that if you get volunteered to coach another season of rec soccer you'll need to up your meds. Whatever the reason, you need to determine if your kid is really ready. Take this test ➤

Multiple-Choice Quiz

Is Your Kid Ready for Club Soccer or the Mob?

1. **When you tell your child it's time to get ready for soccer, they**
    A. Are already dressed, packed, and waiting for you in the car.
    B. Cry with joy and excitement.
    C. Cry.
    D. Puncture the tires on your car.

2. **When your child is on the field during the play of game, they usually**
    A. Have the ball.
    B. Want the ball.
    C. Are watching the ball.
    D. Bury the ball.

3. **When your child has the ball in a game and another player takes it away, they**
    A. Get the ball back.
    B. Trip the other player to get the ball back.
    C. Trip the other player for the fun of it.
    D. Look like they're plotting something.

Programs

4. **Your child spends their free time**
    A. Watching professional soccer.
    B. Mastering soccer moves.
    C. Mastering FIFA career mode.
    D. Masterminding an underground gambling ring.

5. **Your child's soccer bag contains**
    A. Muscle tape, bandages, IcyHot, backup shin guards, and a ball pump.
    B. Their entire uniform and some of their teammates'.
    C. Their Pokémon collection.
    D. Their *Godfather* movie collection.

Interpret Your Score:
Mostly As—Get out your wallet.
Mostly Bs—Cancel all your non-soccer plans.
Mostly Cs—Maybe try next year.
Mostly Ds—Maybe try witness protection.

Rec Coaches

Does your child want to play on the rec team? Yes? Are you sure? Congratulations, now you're the coach. Resist all you want. This. Is. Happening.

When you politely explain that you work full-time, have three kids, deliver meals to senior citizens one day a week, have a severe grass allergy, and have never played soccer before, they will swear to you that it's really no big deal and that you are definitely more qualified than all the other parents, who, you will learn later, all said no. All you have to do, they'll say, is reach out to welcome your players, choose days/times to hold practices (if you want to hold them), give everyone the game schedule, and show up. Honestly, that's it.

	REC TEAM	CLUB TEAM
Getting In	Sign up	Try out
Fees	Less than a trip to the grocery	More than a trip to Disney
Practices	Maybe	2–5 times a week
Game Cadence	Every so often, provided the weather is pleasant	Whenever they're not practicing
Travel	Neighboring subdivisions or communities	Neighboring states or time zones
Tournaments	Um, no	Mother's Day, Memorial Day, Labor Day...
Parent Expectations	Volunteer to coach, bring team snack on assigned day	Get there on time, shut your piehole
Uniform	Jersey donated by local auto repair shop	Car payment territory

Programs

12 THINGS THEY DON'T TELL YOU ABOUT BEING THE REC COACH

1. For the first four weeks of the season, all the kids will look alike.

2. Three players will have the same first name.

3. Half the parents "don't give two shits" about the organization's commitment to letting every kid play at least half of every game, and will text you 1) during the game, 2) on your way home, and/or 3) at work the next day to tell you that your outrageous decision to put Britney/Brittany/Brittnee/Britannie/ Ryan A./Ryan R./Rye/Rhys on the field is the reason you lost the game and don't you think it would be better for all the kids if they won once in a while?

4. Your soccer team includes four kids who can't always be there because they also play basketball; three who always leave early because they play hockey; two who arrive late because of piano lessons; one who just 100 percent does not want to be there; and on any given game day, a handful who have too much homework, an orthodontist appointment, a trip to Grandma's, or no way to get to the field.

5. You will quickly regret your idea of letting the kids choose the team name when, at the first game, you have to lead the cheer, "Go, Green & Purple Dragon Zombie Doughnut Unicorn Sharks!"

6. Your own child will hate you for being the coach because they never get to play as much as everyone else and always has to haul the equipment from your car to the field and back.

7. The other parents will hate you for always favoring your child and giving them more playing time than everyone else.

8. During a meeting at work your boss will call on you while you are busy sketching that night's lineup on the back of the employee charitable giving payroll deduction form she gave you when you walked in the room.

SURVIVING SOCCER

9. The first time you lose your cool it will be because a player on your team has physically or mentally wandered off the field in pursuit of a rabbit hopping behind the goal, a grandparent who came with a sandwich bag full of candy for them, an ice cream truck, or a rainbow.

10. The second time you lose your cool it will be at the other team's coach, who will have either cheated, run up the score, or shown up wearing an adult-sized version of the team's jersey, with "World's Best Coach" printed on the back.

11. You'll have a favorite kid and it will not be your own.

12. At the last game, you'll find out that you've been calling your favorite kid by the wrong name the entire season.

Club Coaches

Most club programs require their coaches, to whom they pay actual money, to hold certain levels of licensing. From the rudimentary I-know-what-I'm-doing-out-there D license up through the I'm-qualified-to-send-kids-to-the-pros A license, club coaches are trained and certified to do their job. Most played through high school, college, and sometimes in a professional league. Clubs like to tout these credentials, so check out the staff page of their websites.

But their heavily acronymed and alphanumeric levels of qualification won't answer the question you really need to ask: is he *the one*?

Can you picture him at your side for the next decade, helping you mold your child into the next USA National Team darling, the next top draft pick, the next Europe-may-offer-more-options player? You need to know if this can work.

Okay, *now* you can Google. But. Just like with any search, you need to be prepared for the results. You're likely to see the pic his younger brother posted of him at his cousin's bachelor party, the crazy road trip story he got tagged in, the selfie his girlfriend took of the two of them at a political rally, the newspaper article about the nasty, career-ending injury he got in his first professional game, and, most unsettling, which other parents already follow him on social media, like all his posts, and leave lengthy, you-are-God's-soccer-gift-to-our-children comments right out there where every other parent can see them. How is this information going to make you feel, and what are you going to do with it?

Want to really know if this guy has what it takes to go the distance with you? If he's sharp enough to recognize your child's gift for the beautiful game? If he possesses the foresight, temperament, and connections to help turn your child into a soccer star? Take this test ▶

True/False Quiz
Club Coach or Mr. Darcy in a Tracksuit?

1. He yells more than you do. (T) (F)

2. You've never seen him without his sunglasses on. (T) (F)

3. His sunglasses are more expensive than yours. (T) (F)

4. He speaks English with a British accent. (T) (F)

5. He speaks English with an Eastern European accent. (T) (F)

6. He participates in drills and scrimmages during practice. (T) (F)

7. He could be a part-time model. (T) (F)

8. He is a part-time model. (T) (F)

9. You have never received a coherent email or text response from him. (T) (F)

10. You have never received any email or text response from him. (T) (F)

11. He's been thrown out of a game by a ref. (T) (F)

12. He wears three-quarters-length track pants. (T) (F)

13. He calls them men's capris. (T) (F)

14. He screams rhetorical questions at the players during games. (T) (F)

15. When he speaks to you, you always turn around to see whom he's really talking to. (T) (F)

Interpret Your Score

13+ True: Save your kid's first pair of cleats. They'll be worth a lot someday.
9–12 True: D1? D2? D3?
5–8 True: You should already be looking into private coaches for supplemental training.
0–4 True: You should introduce him to your single friends instead.

SURVIVING SOCCER

CHAPTER 2

Tryouts

*Beware of advice, like which field your kid should report to
(or how awesome you'd look with bangs).*

How to Inflame Your Kid's Insecurities in 5 Seconds or Less

Some things your kid just has to do on their own. It's tough, but you get
used to it. Plus, it means you're crossing into a new, exciting stage of
parenting, the land of advice-giving and pep talks. Tryouts is the perfect time to dig out the words that will soothe and comfort, embolden
and motivate them. Just know this: it's not about one big spiel. It's an
ongoing rat-a-tat-tat of verbal engagement and confirmation.

Don't worry, you were made for this. After all, who knows your kid's
insecurities better than you?

- Empower them with the responsibility of being in charge of
  their cleats, shin guards, water, EpiPen, and inhaler. Be sure
  to ask them if they have them at least nine times on the way to
  tryouts.

- Build up their resilience by reminding them that no matter how hard they work, it's possible they won't make the team.
- Help them relax with the latest stories of unrest in the Middle East.
- Keep things from getting too quiet in the car. Try:
    - "I hope I got the right day. It was Tuesday, not Monday, right?"
    - "Yikes, look at all that traffic. We may not get there on time."
    - "I don't know, this road just doesn't seem right to me. I hope we're going the right way."
    - "Honey, what's the name of that tall kid, the one who scored all those goals when you played them last season? Abdi's mom said they're coming to your tryouts this year."
    - "Boy, we sure are low on gas! I hope we have enough to get there."
    - "Oh, *that's* where that yarn store is!"
- Make sure they're comfortable by asking them if they need to go potty when, and only when, you're within earshot of all the other kids at the registration table.
- Leave them on a high note. Shout, "I love you, Superstar!" so they can hear you over the coaches and other kids as they're walking away with them.

Welcome to the Counterculture

Your child's club tryout will likely consist of two 90-minute sessions. These three hours will be unlike just about any other experience you'll have as a Soccer Parent. Everything is at stake and nothing is what it seems.

Bring the Antacid

Nerves. Stomachache. Speculation. Worry. Like every parent, you're going to be a wreck. Did you complete the online sign-up form correctly? Did you bring the right paperwork? Do you need their original birth certificate or is a copy okay? Is the photograph they asked you to bring too big or too old? Do you have the right day? The right park? The right time? Will they keep going if it rains? Will they keep going if there is a massive flood? Will that really good kid from the other club come and steal your kid's spot? Will that mom with whom you lost your cool two years ago be there? Will you pretend like you can't see her, or confront her with the  witty retort you've been chewing on all this time? Is your kid really ready? Do they understand how serious these 90 minutes are? Do they have their inhaler? Did they drink enough water over the last couple days? Will they goof off when they see their friends there? Wait, do they really have their inhaler? How many kids will show up in their age group and how many spots are there? Does your outfit look like you're trying too hard, or can you pull off that casual, I'm-not-worried-about-this vibe?

Braggy Daddy or Thanos? Which Dad Are You?

Dressed in work clothes with the faint whiff of car air freshener, these are vastly different versions of the men you saw over the weekend at the last game of the season, losing their shit with a) the ref, b) their kid, or

c) someone else's kid. They stand in a cluster as casual as a backyard barbecue. No sign of the flagrant hostility they displayed just 48 hours earlier over that ball that may or may not have rolled over a line painted in the grass and who touched it last. They will have finally stopped talking about that gross miscarriage of justice, and are now likely talking about a) their personal relationship with the coach, b) their lawn, c) what they're grilling tonight, or d) football.

Pro Tip: Dads, when talk turns to the tryout itself, you've got two ways to play this:

1. Demonstrate your nonchalance by mentioning how the director of another club—just casually drop that he's your neighbor if he lives in your ZIP code—has been begging you to let your daughter play on his top team. It's a quick way to ignite both jealousy and despair in a way that lets you dominate the rest of the conversation, which you can steer in whatever direction you choose.

or

2. Complain disgustedly about how terrible your daughter has been playing recently, only scoring three times in every game, and how you barely let her come to tryouts because you weren't convinced she'd actually take them seriously. This gives them a false sense of superiority and ease, and establishes underdog status for your kid, just in case.

SURVIVING SOCCER

The Dark Side of Capri Town
A One-Act Exploration of Maternal Love

A comfortable distance from the dads, the moms have waded up to the hems of their capris in gossip. It's all they can do to alleviate the discomfort of the moment. And, in some twisted way, sharing gossip feels useful. It's what you do when there's nothing you can do. And, like an end-of-season potluck, everyone brings a dish. So, of course, you should too.

Pro Tip: This is not run-of-the-mill office rumor–mongering, HOA hearsay, or PTA scuttlebutt. It's about your kid's soccer career. You need to nail it. Let everyone else go first. Then, watch the conversation unfurl. Like a game of double-dutch, you have to pay attention to the movement, see the patterns, feel the tempo, and then you can jump in.

"I heard last week that they're making big changes for next year. I think they're going to smaller teams, so I told Geoffrey he'll probably get cut."

"Well, when I brought my famous Texas sheet cake and a donation for the club to buy all new goals and nets over to the director's house last night, he said they're actually expanding the program, creating more spots."

"Coach said to rest this weekend, but Josh really wanted to practice corner kicks, so we hired the assistant coach of the U.S. Men's National Team to do a Zoom session with him at the park."

"Really? I'll never forgive myself for leaving town this weekend for my father-in-law's funeral. Michael wanted to practice so bad, but there just wasn't time. Oh, my god, now I am totally freaking out. What if he is completely flat after not playing for 48 hours?"

Tryouts

"Has anyone seen Barb? She told me she'd be here with Sam, but she also said she'd bring fruit kabobs to the end-of-season party, and we all know how that turned out. I bet they're at another tryout tonight. I knew they weren't happy with Coach this season. She's been complaining that he doesn't have what it takes."

"Oh, they are. Club United's tryouts started at 5:00 PM, so I took a little detour on our way here and drove through the parking lot. Actually, it took a couple passes, but with binoculars I eventually spotted her blue Prius in the corner."

"But who will score goals for us without Sam?"

"Sam's not trying out? Oh, thank God! I mean, well, that's one more spot open for Blake to get into. I'm so worried he'll get cut this year, especially after Tim took Coach on that exclusive fishing charter to talk about Blake getting more playing time and Coach didn't catch anything."

"I don't think Coach is coming back next season, so Blake's going to be fine. I'm worried about Nick because Coach loved him, and if he's gone, who knows what they'll do with Nick! I've been thinking about hiring a publicist for Nick, what do you think? Am I crazy?"

"I saw on Facebook that Sam twisted his ankle this weekend. Maybe that's why he's not here."

"Barb probably just said that so no one thinks he's trying out somewhere else."

SURVIVING SOCCER

> *"Or maybe they're just busy tonight and will come to tomorrow's session. I mean, we can't make it tomorrow night. We have a...thing."*

> *"Wow, I'm not sure what to do now. Should I text the director right now or wait until midnight when I can't sleep? Maybe I'll just swing by tomorrow with some tacos."*

Kids Being Kids

Once enough kids show up, they begin to feel the gravitational pull of each other and start to detach from parents and form little packs of their own. Embrace it. This is a natural migration, and it beats the eyeroll you'd get if you told them to go find their friends.

For boys' tryouts, clusters of five to 10 kids sprout throughout the waiting area. They stand in squished-up circles, massive backpacks slung over one shoulder, making fun of each other. Inadvertently, the boys start knocking a soccer ball back and forth at close range, which means it will ricochet off someone's foot or shin guard and hit one poor boy in the balls. Happens. Every. Time.

At girls' tryouts, you can still expect the clusters, except we call them "mobs." Instead of insults, the talk is louder and filled with adoration, like who is the awesomest player, who has the tryout in the bag, and whose braid is a-mazing. Soccer ball injuries are still in the mix, but it's because the shortest girl in the group is always standing on one—*in her cleats*—so it's never long before she slips off and brings at least two other girls down to the cement with her.

Tryouts

15 Ways to Get the Coach's Attention
While He's Evaluating Your Kid

Once the coach or club director calls all the kids over to the field to begin the tryout, your job is pretty much done. Now you can stay and measure your penis against the other dads, gossip with the moms, run your errand, read your book, or if you're really invested, you can dig in. Grab your binoculars, a notebook, and pen, and let's go.

Now some clubs will post signs that say, **PLAYERS AND COACHES ONLY BEYOND THIS POINT**. Obviously, those signs weren't meant for you. Hitch the canvas strap of your chair over your shoulder and trudge right past them. First of all, who's really going to stop you? And second, you'll be a hero to all the other parents who secretly want to watch too. They'll follow right along. Just walk with authority.

After a warm-up and a quick skill session, tryouts look like a regular soccer game. Feel free to act as you would at a typical match. Just remember, there's a lot more on the line than any old game. Muttering under your breath won't cut it here. Make sure your kid can really hear you. Consider such comments as:

1. "Come *on*, already!"
2. "Air ball!"
3. "Are your eyes open?!"
4. You're going the wrong way!"
5. "Remember, you'll get $20 for each goal you score!"
6. "Are you going to let that kid beat you every time?"
7. "Stop touching your hair!"
8. "Your shoes are untied!"
9. "Stop watching, this isn't YouTube!"
10. "Shoot! Shoot! Shoot! Jesus, what are you waiting for?!"

SURVIVING SOCCER

11. "You had one job!"
12. "Make the run now! Just like we practiced!"
13. "Do you even want this?!"
14. "What are you thinking?!"
15. "Grandma Margie can kick the ball harder than that!"

Do not be dissuaded by your kid's eye rolls. You've got a job to do here and you need to stay focused. Not only will your comments influence how your kid plays, but the coaches will understand your passion and commitment to your child's success as well.

OFFER DAY
A Limited Series in 27 Texts

Before you leave tryouts, make sure you know when offers go out. They are typically issued at a very specific time, like Sunday at 2:00 PM, for example. This is now the most important thing on your calendar.

A note of caution: your text group of parent friends may normally be super helpful, but remember, nothing is normal during tryouts—and that includes offer day. Even though a week ago your kids were battling side by side in the league final, right now your kids are locked in battle over a limited number of spots on the same roster. While normally helpful, group texts can be dangerous on offer day. If you can't hack it, turn off notifications and rehearse a story about how you dropped your phone in the toilet.

Rebecca

It's 2pm!!!

2:00

Rebecca

Haven't gotten anything! Anyone else heard yet????

2:01

Tryouts

Julie
> Yes! Leo just got his! He made it back on the gold team! 2:05

Rebecca
> CONGRATS TO LEO!!!! WOO-HOO!!! 2:06

Rebecca
> Still nothing! 2:10

Tina
> Stop worrying, he's fine! 2:12

Stacy
> Just got ours. Jacob's in. 2:15

Rebecca
> YEAH JACOB!!!!!!!! 2:16

Rebecca
> Why haven't we gotten ours???? I'm literally freaking out! 2:20

SURVIVING SOCCER

Tina

It's fine, we haven't gotten it either. Relax!

2:21

Rebecca

Still nothing! They must have cut Bryan from the club completely. What are we going to do???? I can't stand it!!!!

2:40

Rebecca

Do you think I should call Coach Mike? Maybe he knows something? OMG, Bryan will just die if he doesn't make it!

2:45

Julie

I wouldn't call now. Mike must be swamped. I'm sure you'll hear soon.

2:48

Rebecca

Okay, it's more than an hour late!!!!

3:01

Julie

Technically it was "any time after 2pm," still plenty of time, R

3:03

Rebecca

THANK GOD!!!! FINALLY!!! Bryan's in!!!! He made the team!!!!! I just can't believe it! I can't freaking believe it!!!!

3:10

Tina

Still haven't heard anything here. Keep your finger's crossed.

3:14

Julie

Hang in there, T. I'm sure he's fine.

3:35

Tina

Well, ladies, we finally got Nathan's offer—for the silver team. We'll miss you all on gold!

6:43

Tryouts

Julie

Oh, T, I'm so sorry! That's rotten! N should be on gold! What will we do without him?!

7:20

Tina

Apparently he's not good enough for gold anymore.

7:21

Tina

So much for all the times Coach Mike said what a strong player he was.

7:25

Tina

Maybe they were stringing him along the whole time just to get our money until someone better came along.

7:28

Tina

I'm so mad. I can't believe this. It is so unfair to Nathan.

7:44

Tina

Texted Mike. Keep you posted.

8:12

Tina

Called Mike. No answer. I can't believe this. He never liked Nathan.

8:55

Tina

This is cr*p. I'm going to call Mike at work tomorrow.

9:43

CHAPTER 3

Parent Roles

You've been promoted. New title. More work. And they charge you for it.

Congratulations. You made the team. Your kid, too, of course. This is officially a family affair. Now, before you buy their cleats, and before they pick out the number that will get ironed on their jersey, doodled in their notebook, and mowed into your front lawn, you need to do something. Get in your car. Really sit in it. Just sit there. Like it's a chair you're not getting out of for the next 10 years. Then take a hard look in the rearview mirror and ask yourself this question: Are you up for this?

Can you be the Soccer Parent your kid needs you to be? Are you ready for hours of driving and loads of laundry? Blistery feet and blustery moods? Gas station dinners and the perpetual dread that you've forgotten something essential? The truth is, this job isn't something you do, it's someone you are.

If you don't see a Soccer Parent in the reflection, all is not lost. You've read this far, so you're in striking distance. Besides, being the half-baked alternative—the Parent Whose Kid Plays Soccer—just isn't a good look.

SOCCER PARENT VS. PARENT WHOSE KID PLAYS SOCCER

Soccer Parent

- Perfect game attendance
- Most likely to get their kid—and anyone else's—to the right location at the right time
- Can name every player's parents, siblings, grandparents, and pets
- Calls the academy scout by his first name
  - ⊛ *Haunts his favorite coffee shop*
  - ⊛ *Macchiato, two sugars*
- Accurately predicts which parent will get thrown out of a game first
- Can detect coach's mood based on whether he's standing, pacing, or crouching
- No. 1 at insulting the referees
- Best comebacks to opposing fans' taunts
- Always knows the score
- Never called any of the identical twins by the wrong name
- Achieved total mastery of the season's schedule

Parent Whose Kid Plays Soccer

- "Which one's the coach?"
- "Did we win?"
- "Foul ball!"
- "Is there a game today? What time?"
- "Carpool? What carpool?"
- "Just explain to your coach that you won't be at practice tonight because Mercury is in retrograde."
- "No, you didn't reach me at a bad time, Aunt Sheila. I'm just at Henry's soccer game. Sure, this is a perfect time to tell me about your knee replacement. Hold on, my hands are full, let me put you on speaker."
- "Is No. 8 a boy or a girl? I just can't tell."

SURVIVING SOCCER

I Interrupt This Book for a Very Important Message

It's hardly been enough time to clear last season's shin guard smell out of your car when the email arrives. It's the one your kid's new coach sends just before the season begins, and it's got a lot of "Rah-rah-rah, it's gonna be a great season" talk, "Here's the league we're playing in" info, "Here's what I'm gonna do for our team" overly ambitious goals, and "Here's what I expect from the players" guidelines. This is the most you will hear from the coach in every interaction the entire season. Combined. And, buried beneath all the coaching mumbo-jumbo is the zinger: the request for a volunteer team administrator.

Now, you need to be extra careful here. Expose any vulnerability, and you'll be locked in like a Cancun timeshare.

Do not raise your hand to be the admin. Do not be distracted by the coach's warm welcome and openness. Do not be persuaded by his inspiring words. Do not be deceived into thinking volunteering to be the admin will set a good example of teamwork for your kid. Do not let your guilt about not making your child's baby food from scratch cloud your judgment. And, most importantly, do not be deluded enough to believe that being the admin will help you advance your child's sports career.

The temptation will be there.

This email will make you feel informed, empowered, and inspired about the season ahead, but it's just a ruse. Do not reply to say thank you for having Johnny on your team, to say how excited you are for the upcoming season, or, heaven forbid, to politely inquire about the time commitment of being the admin. This entire email is a trap. The kind you can't get out of without chewing off a limb.

Don't believe me? Then clear your schedule for:

- Hours of collecting, organizing, and submitting birth certificates, liability waivers, and spirit wear orders
- Logistical acrobatics—Cirque du Soleil–level—of scheduling and paying referees
- Technological wizardry of managing the team's calendar, roster, and communications
- Troubleshooting for all the parents who can't figure out the team scheduling app
- Texts, emails, phone calls, sideline questions, and grievances from other parents

Maybe it's already too late. Maybe the coach already thanked you for volunteering even though you definitely, absolutely 100 percent don't *think* you volunteered. Start practicing the poker face you'll need when you pick the restaurant for the team dinner. Half the parents will think you made a terrible choice while the other half will tell you to your face.

A better option is to direct your energy into becoming the admin's best friend. Know their coffee order, remember their player's name, and offer them your extra umbrella, blanket, portable battery charger, or *Hamilton* tickets.

Why bother? Imagine this:

- Early access to crucial information, like schedule changes and team gossip
- A direct but anonymous line of contact to the coach for all of your complaints
- A direct but impartial line of contact to the coach to remind him that your child is the best player on the team
- Someone to sit next to at games who won't bore you with anything that isn't related to your kids' soccer team

SURVIVING SOCCER

THE ADMIN'S PHONE IS A DUMPSTER FIRE
Previously Unreleased Screenshots

> Why is the practice field so far away from our house?

> We have a big yard. Could you ask the coach to have practice at our place?

> My yoga class ran late. Will you bring Sebastian home?

> The practice time is too early and it interrupts our dinner.

> Practice starts too late. We have to rush dinner.

> Why are there so many practices each week?

> Why aren't there more practices each week?

> Could you please tell the coach to play my daughter on the left side of the field so she can hear me better during the game?

> Practices are too short.

> Practices are too long.

> Why didn't my son play in the second half last night? I got to the game late and didn't even get to see him play.

> Please tell the coach that our soccer consultant said our son needs more game time.

> My daughter doesn't have enough time to do her homework because of soccer.

> My son has to leave early on Tuesdays and Wednesdays because of hockey practice.

Parent Roles

> My son will be late for the first three weeks because of baseball practice.

> My daughter's basketball coach doesn't want her to play more than 25 minutes during any soccer game.

> I have other children on other teams who practice at other locations at the same time, so I can't promise my son will always be there.

> I can't get my son to practices on Tuesdays, Wednesdays, or alternating Thursdays, and honestly, Fridays would work a lot better for our family. If that's okay.

For those of you who take this sage advice and strategically worm your way out of becoming the team admin, first of all, you're welcome. And congratulations! You now have an extra 15 hours a week to spend plotting, coordinating, drafting, re-drafting, triple-checking, and second-guessing all your own communications with the coach. You're going to need it.

10 Things That Happen While You Wait for the Coach to Text You Back

You know it's a bad idea. And yet you're going to do it anyway. We all do. At some point during the season—let's face it, at many points during the season—you're going to ~~want to~~ feel the scorching desire to communicate with your kid's coach about one of the three topics he has made you swear *never* to talk to him about: your child's playing time, your child's position on the field, or his coaching.

 SURVIVING SOCCER

Your message will feel important. Dire even. As you consider the urgent nature of what you have to say/ask/plead, you'll remember that you have the coach's cell number committed to memory from that time you overheard him giving it to the dad of the kid who was hauled off the field on a stretcher.

After you polish the 19th draft of your one-sentence text, close your eyes, say a prayer, and hit send, expect to find yourself doing the following:

1. Closing and reopening your text app.
2. Switching from your text app to your favorite game and beating your all-time high score.
3. Taking your phone off vibrate and turning the volume up to high.
4. Googling how to unsend a text.
5. Restarting your phone.
6. Reexamining your life choices.
7. Closing and reopening your text app again.
8. Screaming into a pillow.
9. Sending a "test" text to your best friend to make sure your phone is working.
10. Googling "best countries for expats with families."

Analyze the Coach's Email Like an English Major

There may come a time when you're casually cleaning out your inbox, deleting all the emails with last-minute fare alerts and the passive-aggressive updates from the neighborhood social media platform, when it appears. Just like opening the dryer and finding a very clean $20 bill, at the top of your inbox is a message from the coach. You may need to blink a few times to make sure you're seeing what you think you're seeing. Once you confirm it's not a mirage, it's time to get to work. Channel your inner 12-year-old because you can't just read this email, you have to examine it from every perspective, like a middle school crush.

What you can assume based on when he sent the email:
- A weekend, early morning timestamp means the coach was watching the 7:00 AM match between Manchester City and Liverpool, with some of the best players in the English Premier League, and it made him think of your kid's vast potential.
- A weekday, office-hours timestamp means the coach interrupted a very important meeting during his day job because he couldn't stop thinking about that play your kid made in the game last night and needed to congratulate you about it.
- A weekday, 5:00–6:00 PM timestamp probably means the coach of the academy team needs a last-minute replacement for his roster and asked your coach to reach out to his best player.
- A 9:00 PM–6:00 AM timestamp on any day means your child is so good that visions of their greatness permeate the coach's subconsciousness during the only times he's not thinking about the team.

How to interpret the subject line:
- No good coach has time in his life to bother with writing a subject line.
- Your coach wrote a subject line? Let go of those scholarship dreams right about now.

What the salutation means:
- If the email begins with anything remotely formal, like DEAR, TO, or even HELLO, you can stop right there. This email is likely about

38   SURVIVING SOCCER

the outstanding balance of your soccer fees or the snack calendar that you have yet to add your name to.

- Emails that start with HEY— or YO! are like gift-wrapped presents that have a good heft to them. Chances are you're going to like what's inside.
- No salutation? This is a best-case scenario. Your kid is so staggeringly impressive that niceties are ridiculous in light of the closeness you two will have as he helps launch your kid's soccer career.

Style and tone watch-outs:

- Be cautious if you detect too much kindness. This means he wants something and it might just be your help coordinating a gift for the team administrator.
- Humor is a major red flag. Coaches are not funny.
- Impersonal is not as bad as it may sound. He's probably trying to play down the fact that he invited professional scouts to the next game to watch your kid.
- Optimism comes right out of the coaching playbook. It's their default mode. Don't read anything into it.
- Irritation is also in the coaching playbook. It's their other default mode. Nothing to get excited or worry about.
- Abrupt and littered with acronyms, abbreviations, and contractions means he's likely excited about your child's future. Congratulations.

A primer on coaches' grammar and punctuation:

- Listen, your coach has more important things to worry about than where commas go and whether or not i comes before e.

Parent Roles

- Assume that the more typos you find, the more ecstatic he is about sending a message to the adult responsible for giving him his favorite player.
- Any coach who has the time to proofread his emails before hitting send isn't putting the kind of energy into the game that your kid needs to be successful.

The sign-off explained:

- *See* salutations: tl;dr—less is best.

How to Deal When You Get Texts from Parents You Don't Know

+1 (614) 555-1234 >

Hi!! We have Caitlyn's warm-up jacket!? House key in pocket!! Find me at practice.

Here it is. The moment you've been dreading. A text from another parent on your team, and you have no idea who it is.

This is the perfect time to panic. But your deductive reasoning has gotten you this far. Remember, you once located field D-17 Blue at a 400-acre sports complex with five entrances and a field map from 2013.

Just take a closer look at that message. It's full of clues.

 SURVIVING SOCCER

Start with a deep dive into punctuation:

1. Since the text actually has punctuation, you can eliminate the two sets of parents who you thought were way too young to have a kid the same age as yours.
2. The exclamation points scream (literally) that your sender is high-energy. At some point, they told you what they thought was a totally hilarious story about washing their kid's jersey with bar soap in a hotel room sink at a tournament, accidentally driving to the wrong field, or dropping their phone in a porta john.
3. Rule out the mom who sits at the end of the sideline and never speaks. Punctuation, like conversation with other Soccer Parents, is beneath her.
4. Note the double-marking of sentences. Two consecutive exclamation points equals high-energy with caffeine on top. Which parent is always calculating whether they can make it to Starbucks and back before kickoff? Also, look closely at any parent who has ever high-fived you during a game or brought a cowbell.

Now let's get to the meat (stick) and potato (chips) of the message. You don't need Nicolas Cage, lemon juice, and a hairdryer to decipher it. This parent went through your kid's pockets. You don't even go through your kid's pockets. Your sender is telling you that they have a loose relationship with rules and what appears to be a low threshold for self-preservation. You're looking for someone who makes their own parking spot. Someone who "forgot" to put their name on the snack calendar. Someone who boasts about ignoring the $20-a-pair field sock requirement for a $1.19 bag of plain white tube socks from Walmart. Also probably someone who scrounges dinner out of their glove box.

Parent Roles

By now you've cut the roster in half. Use your gut to knock three or four more names off the list. Start with families that have more kids than adults—they don't have time to go through their kids' soccer bags. Then cross off the parent who would just keep the jacket because their kid has likely already lost theirs.

You should be down to four people, max. Either use your favorite multiple-choice test-taking strategy, or go on offense:

1. If your team has a heavy car culture—parents who sit in their vehicles doing work or doom-scrolling during practice—try something simple, like, "Which car did you take today?" Never mind that true soccer families have a designated soccer car.

2. If your team's parents stand outside and gossip during practice, no hiding in the back of your minivan with your iPad and a bag of Twizzlers. You need to participate and you need something juicy. It doesn't matter if it's true. Remember, this is self-preservation. In fact, you need to make an entrance—no slipping in quietly. Make sure everyone sees you're there so your texter comes to you first. That's right, draw them out.

3. If any type of social interaction is off the table, feel free to play the UNO reverse card. "Caitlynn will learn to live without her jacket. I'm teaching her to keep track of her own things. Maybe you should try it."

4. If you want to make this the last text you ever receive from another Soccer Parent, choose the nuclear option: "I'm sure Caitlynn's warm-up just FELL into your kid's bag by ACCIDENT. Unless you want me to alert the club director, I expect to find her jacket washed, folded, and sitting on my porch by sunrise." Don't bother including your address because now it's their turn to squirm.

SURVIVING SOCCER

Free Time—How to Master the Art of Doing Nothing (The Ugly Off-Season)

Ready to get sucked into the cyclone that will be your soccer schedule? Hold your horses. Let's not overlook the significance of the off-season first. Don't be fooled into thinking this is just when your kid isn't playing soccer. Technically, yes, your kid isn't doing anything. But that's only what it looks like. It's what you say to other parents—especially those whose kids don't do extracurriculars—that makes all the difference.

Remember, parenting is its own sport. Everyone keeps score. And while it seems natural to measure the success of the soccer season by how many wins your kid has, you've got to think about the off-season the same way.

That's because doing nothing can be measured, judged, and even celebrated as much as doing something. Take baseball. Parents of ball-players are pros at this. There's their kid standing at bat. The pitcher throws the ball. Maybe it sails into the strike zone or maybe it falls 20 feet short. Maybe their kid makes a keen judgment not to swing, or maybe their eyes are glued shut. So long as they just stand there doing absolutely nothing, parents will shout, "Good eye!" with the boisterous, atta-boy pride and enthusiasm that they only use when other people are around.

So, the next time someone hopelessly confesses the outrageous number of hours their kid spends bingeing on all the screens they bought for them but wish they wouldn't use, hold off on the feel-good commiseration they're looking for. Throw them a curveball instead.

Tell them you're giving your kid some much-deserved downtime. Say it like they're LeBron after carrying his team through the playoffs, like you're enforcing strict R&R because that's what good parents do.

Parent Roles

Added bonus: your non-soccer friends and family will feel like you finally heard their unsolicited remarks about overscheduling.

It's not hard to convince other parents how important downtime is and how you're doing right by your kid by locking down his calendar for a while. But the key is not letting those parents see—or smell—the truth.

Okay, listen. This is some NDA-level info. And if it gets out, it's bad for all of us. See, downtime is more than just pressing pause for a couple months on the games, training, and all that super-healthy eating you pretend happens during the season. The off-season means not rushing around all the time (read: being late to everything). You'll be amazed at how far your kid's grades can fall and how fast, with all that time to study. And there will be naps. Lots of them. Not the good kind. We're talking heavy, drooling, foul-smelling sleep that leaves your kid looking worse than before.

Be prepared to face the laziest, most disgusting version of your kid you've ever seen. For the longest 12 weeks of your life. But that's nothing compared to what it does to your own productivity level. Listen up. You need to get your life in order now, while you can. Pay your taxes. Order your turkey. Schedule the air-duct cleaners. Wish everyone you care about a happy birthday. Because the off-season starts with all the momentum of hitting a parked car. You'll be shocked by the impact, distraught by the damage, and pissed off because you should have totally seen it coming.

SURVIVING SOCCER

Charting Parent Productivity Levels by Season

Daily Parent Productivity: Peak Soccer Season

- Run 10k before sunrise.
  - Meditate.
    - Pull lettuce, carrots, cukes, and radishes from the garden to pack easy lunch salad.
    - Complete 10-hour workday.
    - Be first in line for after-school pickup.
    - Mail gift to college friend in plenty of time for birthday.
- Mow lawn.
- Mow neighbor's lawn.
- Cook new recipe from *Easy Weeknight Dinners with 24 Ingredients or Less*.
- Get a cut, color, keratin treatment, and blowout.
- Re-stock your Etsy store.
- Hit every green light driving the carpool.
- Dash off a witty tweet that adds 1K+ followers, starts trending, and elicits a follow request from your ex.

  - Gas up.
    - Make invitations for your parents' 50th anniversary party.
    - Admire your spotless mudroom cubbies.
    - Complete school photo order form.
    - Write check for school photos.
  - Put photo order form and check into the right child's backpack.

Parent Roles   45

- Review color-coded schedule on fridge whiteboard and divvy up tomorrow's duties with spouse.
- Moisturize.
- Catch up on last season of *Grey's*.

Daily Parent Productivity: The Off-Season

- Hit a snooze-button record.
- Drop kid at school.
- White-knuckle drive to work.
- Return home to assemble and drop off kid's lunch.
- Get pulled over going 32 in a school zone.
- Eat discarded half of granola bar you found digging out your registration.
- Walk in late to department meeting.
- Notice sticky pieces of granola on shirt.
- Forget to pick up poster board for school project due tomorrow.
- Realize you're out of dog food.
- Head back out at 7:00 PM to Pet Supplies Plus, OfficeMax, Panera, Chipotle, and Taco Bell (because this is who we are now).
- Trip over skateboard when you step inside house.
- Argue with child about email from teacher re: missing reading log.
- Stay up until 11:30 PM "helping" child with poster board project.
- Remember that it is (was) spouse's birthday.
- Doom-scroll until you fall asleep, face on your phone, which you forget to plug into your charger.

46 SURVIVING SOCCER

Here's the good news: just when you think you can't take one more minute of your child's therapeutic off-season downtime, you get the much-anticipated email from your team admin, telling you what your family's life will look like for the next three to four months.

You'll recognize the email when your inbox plays the "Hallelujah Chorus," performed by the Mormon Tabernacle Choir. Now, you're going to be excited about this. However, before you open it, you need to do something. It only takes a minute.

CLEAR YOUR ENTIRE SCHEDULE IN 5 SIMPLE STEPS

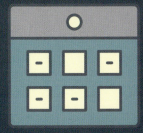

1. Go to your corkboard, fridge, chalkboard wall, island catch-all, and that overgrown pile of super-important pieces of mail you've stashed on that one corner of your kitchen counter.

2. Gather up all the postcard reminders to schedule dental checkups, mammograms, oil changes, rabies shots, and air-duct cleanings.

3. Retrieve all the invitations to weddings, baby showers, surprise parties, and bar/bat mitzvahs that you've been getting around to RSVPing to.

Parent Roles 47

4. Take any other time-sensitive pieces, including, but not limited to the notice for your child's choir concert, your parent-teacher conference reminder, apple-picking dates, concert tickets you bought to surprise your spouse for your anniversary, and a parenting workshop that your child's teacher, school counselor, pediatrician, and hairdresser have strongly recommended you attend.

5. Run over them with the lawn mower.

Now open the email.

PART II

GET TO PRACTICE

CHAPTER 4

Schedules + Punctuality

Repeat after me: "I can't, my kid has practice."

Soccer practices are the packed lunch of soccer season. You will dread them because they never end; your kid will fluctuate between indifference toward them and accusing you of enjoying this "torture"; and, to everyone's dismay, they make up the majority of the season. On the other hand, games—like the school's hot lunches—make the kids happy but are full of things you're probably better off not knowing about.

Practices are the foundation of a kid's soccer experience—socially, emotionally, and athletically. They hijack your weeknight routine, force you into awkward social interactions with other parents, and eat up a lot of gas and time. But, the sooner you come to terms with how important they are and just suck it up and drive the carpool, the better off everyone will be.

So You Think That's Your Schedule
A Game of Chutes and Ladders

In the same way women forget what childbirth—and living with a newborn—is really like long enough to get pregnant and go through it all over again, each year during the couple of months between soccer seasons, you will subconsciously suppress the three most painful things about soccer practice: 1) The field is never close; 2) The timing is never good; 3) The schedule always changes.

As it states in the admin's email, this practice schedule is set for the season and will never change.*

- ★ Mondays, 5:30 PM at Rocky Fields Metro Park
- ★ Wednesdays, 6:45 PM at Ramshackle Heights HS (Go Rams!)
- ★ Thursdays, 6:00 PM at Our Lady in the Middle-of-Nowhere Church

---

*Except when:

- ★ Practice is moved to Saturday at 2:00 PM because they have a game on Thursday.
- ★ Practice is Friday at 7:10 PM at Derelict Park because it's the third week of the month.
- ★ Practice is moved to Too Many Creeks Park because the church is re-paving its parking lot.
- ★ Wednesday's practice is moved to No Saints Middle School because the Rams have a JV football home game.
- ★ Practice is moved to Mosquito's Revenge Park at 5:30 PM, because another team wants to scrimmage your team on Wednesday. Please be there by 5:00 PM at the latest.
- ★ Practice is moved to the upper field (which is technically below the lower field) on the northwest side of Broken Ox Bridge because the church is having a revival.

 SURVIVING SOCCER

- ★ Practice on Wednesday is 7:30–8:00 PM because your coach's other team has a game that night, and the coach who's covering for him is only open then.
- ★ Monday practice is moved to Tuesday, still at Rocky Fields, but at 5:45 PM, because five players on the team have a long-distance field trip for school.
- ★ The city is hosting a Family Fitness Walk that starts at Mama JoJo's Wing Joint on Monday, using Rocky Fields for overflow parking. The practice fields are still available, but the lot will be closed to everyone but the walkers, so parents need to park at Out of Your League Elementary no later than 4:45 PM and then *ride with their kids* on the shuttle the club is providing to Rocky Fields.
- ★ Monday practice is moved to Ramshackle Heights at 7:15 PM because it rained all weekend, so Rocky Fields is closed to prevent damage to the little grass they have.
- ★ The church is having a community-wide outdoor prayer circle, so practice is moved to the parking lot. Be sure to bring tennis shoes or flats, preferably flats, but tennis shoes will do in a pinch.
- ★ Monday's practice is canceled and Wednesday's will start an hour earlier because your coach traveled to Vegas for a buddy's bachelor party over the weekend.

THIS IS IMPORTANT! Practice start time is not the same as practice arrival time. Practice start time is the moment the coach begins the first drill. All players need to be on the field, in their cleats and shin guards, warmed up, hydrated, and done with all fart jokes. Depending on your coach, arrival time is anywhere from 15 to 45 minutes prior to the start time that's actually on the calendar.

Schedules + Punctuality

Get There Less Than an Hour Early, If You Dare
What You Should Really Worry About

Everyone you know who does not have a child who plays soccer will tell you that you need to be afraid of concussions, torn ACLs, muscle overuse, playing when it's too hot, and playing when it's too cold.

Everyone you know who has a child who used to play soccer before they pulled them out because it "wasn't working for their family," will tell you that you really need to worry about reckless competitors, referees who don't call fouls, and coaches who only care about winning.

In reality, there's something much bigger to fear: the clock. Will you get your kid where they need to be, when they need to be there? On top of factoring in your personal brand of punctuality, you've got traffic, construction, schedule changes, and carpool confusion in play. And let's not forget the biggest threat to getting there on time: your spouse, who, deep down, may not be all the Soccer Parent that you are.

When you're carving grooves into your palms with what's left of your nails because a water main break forced you to take a detour that routed you back home, then off in the opposite direction, your spouse may notice the veins bulging out of your neck and very innocently ask you, "So he's a little late, so what?"

So what?

When it comes to punctuality and soccer:

- Early = On time.
- On time = Late.
- Late = Your-parents-obviously-don't-love-you-enough-to-get-you-here-when-you're-supposed-to-be-here-so-you-might-as-well-sit-on-the-bench-for-the-rest-of-the-season.

That's what.

The Bench

A Coach's Secret Weapon

It's all about the bench. It's the coaching equivalent of the Naughty Step. When the coach doesn't like what your kid is doing, he can put him on the bench until he is ready to deal with him. And while your kid waits where the whole world (read: parents) can see him—he's not on the field playing soccer.

For coaches, the bench is a double-threat. First, kids hate the bench. They're on the team because they want to play soccer games, not practice all week, warm up before the match, then sit while their teammates have all the fun and get all the glory.

But kids aren't the only ones thinking about how many minutes they get on the field. Parents count them too. Out loud. In front of everyone. (They are also doing it very privately in angry texts they shoot to the coach before, during, and after the game.)

Minutes are the most powerful currency in this ecosystem. You already know that time is money, but in soccer, that's not all it is. Your pride is at stake too. Coaches know how much your club fees are. Coaches know that you're not paying these fees to watch your kid sit on the bench. And coaches also know that you're not paying these fees to let other parents, who also know how much you're paying, watch you watch your kid sit on the bench. Especially while their kids are zipping up and down the field with the soccer ball.

The coach is no dummy. He knows that if you're hyper-focused in one area, you can't pay much attention to anything else. So by making you irrationally preoccupied with time/transportation, which, honestly, is the only thing in your control anyway, you'll have less energy to criticize him about everything else you're unhappy about.

Why else do you think big clubs require kids to wear training uniforms to practice? They'll tell you it's about being professional and looking like a respectable team. Nonsense. They know exactly how many loads of wash you need to do in order for your kid to have his special training kit—jersey, shorts, and socks—clean for every single practice. You'll be so busy flipping the wash and searching for your kid's missing black sock—the one with two white bands at the top, not three—that you won't have time to email or text him about how your kid would be much better if he played left wing and not right.

CHAPTER 5

Cars + Parking Lots

You will never get that shin guard smell out of your car.

Your Third Place Now Has Four Wheels

Why are Soccer Parents so obsessed with their cars? Because we live in them. The schlep to practice is only the beginning. Consider intrastate and interstate travel for games and tournaments. It's our waiting room, mobile office, coffee shop, rain shelter, changing room, nap nook, breakfast bar, lunch dive, and drive-thru diner. You won't find this on the club website or even during the 30-second gathering after the first practice that the coach will call your "team meeting," but it's important to know where you'll spend your time.

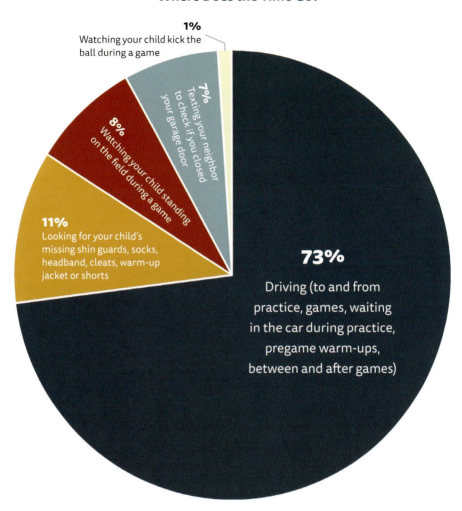

Where Does the Time Go?

- **1%** Watching your child kick the ball during a game
- **7%** Texting your neighbor to check if you closed your garage door
- **8%** Watching your child standing on the field during a game
- **11%** Looking for your child's missing shin guards, socks, headband, cleats, warm-up jacket or shorts
- **73%** Driving (to and from practice, games, waiting in the car during practice, pregame warm-ups, between and after games)

The Nice Car vs. Crappy Car Debate

There are a lot of tools to make your life as a Soccer Parent a lot easier. Waterproof blankets. Insulated rain boots. Ventilated sun hats. Cool cloths. Bug spray. Windscreens. Four-season weather pods. Those little heat packets you can slip into your mittens, pockets, or shoes. But based on the time you're going to spend in your car, that's what we need to talk about first.

Here's what J.D. Power, *Consumer Reports*, and your dad can't tell you about cars. Anyone whose kid plays soccer drives either one of two vehicles, a nice car or a crappy car. Nice/crappy cars come from every manufacturer, in any size, in any price range, and can be any age. Ultimately, you choose which category it fits in. But you should know what you're getting yourself into.

Emotional Bandwidth to Deal with Anything Other Than the Wet, Muddy Kids They Need to Drive Home

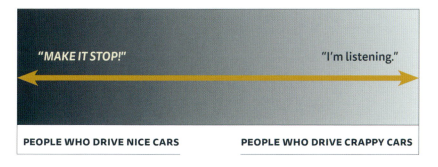

Time Left Each Day After Cleaning Out the Car

PEOPLE WHO DRIVE NICE CARS
You won't even get around to washing last night's dishes.

PEOPLE WHO DRIVE CRAPPY CARS
Par-ty! Just kidding. No one whose kid plays sports has any personal time.

Cars + Parking Lots

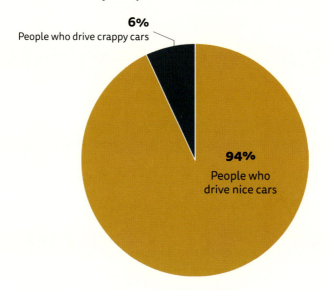

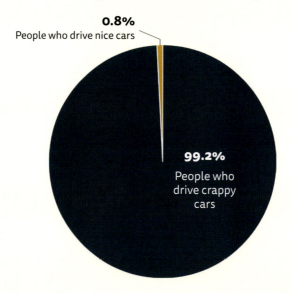

Probability of Finding Something in the Car You Can Safely Eat When Practice Runs Late

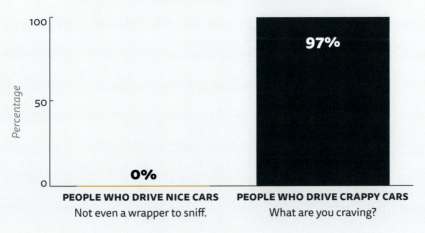

PEOPLE WHO DRIVE NICE CARS — 0%
Not even a wrapper to sniff.

PEOPLE WHO DRIVE CRAPPY CARS — 97%
What are you craving?

Top Reasons for ER Visits (Nice Cars/Crappy Cars)

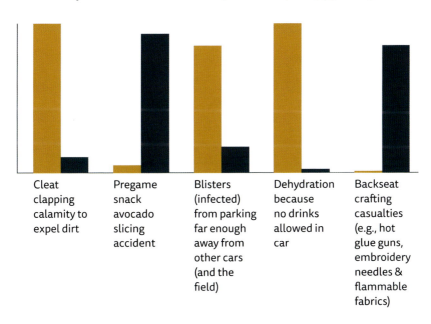

- Cleat clapping calamity to expel dirt
- Pregame snack avocado slicing accident
- Blisters (infected) from parking far enough away from other cars (and the field)
- Dehydration because no drinks allowed in car
- Backseat crafting casualties (e.g., hot glue guns, embroidery needles & flammable fabrics)

Cars + Parking Lots

The Minivan—Meet the Elephant in the Driveway

It's impossible to chart your child's trajectory to soccer stardom without acknowledging the most recognizable and polarizing symbol of Soccer Parents everywhere. The minivan. Call it the Swiss Army Knife of parenting.

For some, no matter where you are or what you need, the solution is in the minivan. You show me a Soccer Parent with a minivan, and I'll show you a person you can rely on when your kid forgets his shin guards, cleats, jersey, water bottle, sunblock, snack, or emergency inhaler.

This beloved storage chariot is like a room in your house you can just take with you. It's part pantry, part toy chest, part linen closet, part media room, part laundry bin, part changing room, and part living room. Being in someone else's minivan is more like a visit to their home than a ride in their car. At first you're flattered by the invitation, but when you settle in your spot, the discarded beef jerky wrappers, bags of clothes marked for Goodwill, partially completed/destroyed shoebox diorama, stack of library books, empty but lived-in birdcage, apple core, and loose needle with thread in the cupholder, you start to wonder whether your shots and will are up to date.

You'd think every Soccer Parent would drive one of these clutter shuttles, but not everyone can pull it off. Not everyone can wrangle this benevolent beast. To the uninitiated, the minivan can feel awkward, unnatural even. Things like entering the vehicle, steering it around parked cars, opening the glove compartment, and pulling into your garage take thoughtful coordination possessed only by a chosen, elite group. It's the fat suit of cars. To drive it you must become it. Embrace the size, assume the power, and enjoy the ride.

Cars + Parking Lots

TINDER PROFILES FOR SOCCER-PARENT CARS

ST33LY

Gravel parking lots don't scare me. Neither do never-washed trunk blankets or fruit snacks left in my cup holders on 100-degree days. Trust me. I've seen things. Show me what you've got.

SP0TLSS

Mileage is just a number. In fact, you won't believe mine when you look under the hood. Lube is my love language. Proud maintenance freak. I dare you to peek beneath my seats. No turf pellets. No Gatorade lids. No granola bits. And, yes, my windows still go up and down.

YRS247

Use me and abuse me. Hang wet field socks on my wipers. Light the pre-dawn field with my headlights. Weigh me down with cases of bottled water. Leave a half-eaten yogurt cup in the backseat all weekend in July. Never wash me. I'm here for all of it.

LIFS4VR

In the zombie apocalypse, I will keep you safe, warm, dry, fed, clothed, entertained, and smelling like shin guards for weeks.

SNKYP3T

Two truths and a lie...I've never gotten a speeding ticket running late to the field. I have my own bay at the garage where I get oil changes. It took my family 17 weeks to discover that their hamster had moved into my trunk.

UNBTHRD

Unpopular opinions...
The referee wasn't the problem.... Yes, your kid was offside.... Backing into a parking spot does not make you a better person.

Road Rules Need Not Apply

Lessons from the Parking Lot

If you find yourself blushing at what some parents say out loud—loudly—on the sideline, brace yourself for the parking lot. Before and after games, this is where real life happens, and it's not pretty. Remember those black-and-white scenes where Dorothy wishes her life in Kansas was different? That's you in the parking lot. Just being real here. That lot gets packed with much more than cars—there's whining, impatience, hangryness, nerves, and failed expectations. And that's just the adults.

On the road, people believe their cars are invisibility cloaks. They think no one really sees them singing, crying, or picking their nose through their clear glass windows, going 10 miles over the speed limit. The parking lot—soccer game purgatory—also gives a false sense of anonymity. But the reality is, even in the Mall of America–sized parking lot of a massive sporting complex on a tournament weekend, most of the people arriving and leaving at the same time as you will more than likely be on your field, if not on your team.

Here's what I've learned from the parking lot:

- Your car may not get keyed, but it will get chaired.
- Fancy SUVs are like push-up bras. They make quite an entrance, but don't always deliver the goods.
- The sketchy looking guy asleep in the beat-up Corolla will most definitely be your ref.
- Parking too close to another car is a sign of dominance—not negligence. Where do you think you are, Target?
- Getting that one shady parking spot in the lot requires *Lord of the Flies*–like behavior, and it's totally worth it.

- In your attempt to carry everything from the lot to the field in one trip, you will not be a good judge of the space you take up. Don't walk within 10 yards of another parent unless you're up to speed on local concealed-carry laws.
- Car stickers with your kid's name and club are the wallet photos of our time. If you don't have one, how do we know you really love them?
- **BEWARE:** Parents giving pregame and postgame lectures will be lurking behind large cars and porta johns. Just jingle your keys so they hear you coming.
- The bigger the vehicle, the more justified people feel letting it obstruct the flow of traffic while they chat with their closest friends.
- The dads who are the most vocal on the sidelines are not the same dads who can help you with your jumper cables.

SURVIVING SOCCER

CHAPTER 6

Driving + Carpools

Enjoy life with a stranger's kid in the backseat.

Let's Talk

The one thing you can count on as a soccer family is that once the season starts, you won't eat a meal together for the next three months. You can dream about what you're missing out on while you imagine all the other families enjoying meaningful, witty dinner conversations over home cooked meals that everyone in the house loves and graciously compliments. Or you can just roll your eyes at your reflection in the microwave while you nuke a Lean Cuisine and enjoy four uninterrupted minutes of Candy Crush as you wolf it down.

What you'll soon learn is that driving is the new dinner. Sure, Soccer Parents complain all day about how much time they spend in the car, how they have to schlep their kids from place to place to place, but it's all a cover. Truth is, the car beats the dinner table every time. Get it right and you can get the goods on your kid—and then pretend-grumble with the rest of us.

The Say-Nothing-Get-Everything Paradox

Want to make this work? Once you're in the car:

1. Keep your mouth shut.
2. Avoid eye contact.
3. Don't play your stupid music.
4. Don't play boring talk radio.
5. Continue to keep your mouth shut.
6. Make believe your kid isn't there.
7. Watch the road and nothing else.

Now, as you patiently tread in the depths of this excruciating quiet, your child will eventually share a thought out loud. This may be while you're backing out of the drive to go to the first practice or halfway through the season. I can't tell you when it will happen, but I can tell you that when it does, you need to be ready. Like a surfer waiting for that longed-for swell of the water, if you're patient—and you have the physical and mental stamina to get yourself upright and balanced at precisely the right moment—you can ride that beautiful wave of conversation and learn what they're thinking about school, friends, and life. Surrender to the deep.

Not that patient? You're not completely out of luck. Remember, your goal here is information, not interaction. Meet your new secret weapon: the carpool.

Discovering the joy of the carpool is a major parenting milestone. You hated it when you were a kid. You were appalled by the idea of it in early adulthood. But just like naps, leftovers, and getting carded, eventually you'll change your mind about the carpool, too—especially on the days someone else drives it.

Carpool Chess

4 Ways to Force Their Moves

When you're building your carpool, go big. We're talking four passengers minimum. You want enough kids in the car that they 1) play off each other's personalities, 2) keep the conversation going even when one kid is out or in a mood, 3) offer a diversity of perspectives, and 4) provide a critical mass for taking sides.

Know your route. By heart. The fewer distractions you have—including your navigation app—the more intel you can absorb. Once every kid is collected and buckled into your car, lock into stealth mode. Like meditation, your success relies on your ability to do absolutely nothing.

THE CARPOOLING PATH TO ENLIGHTENMENT

Level 1: Consciousness

Welcome. The information you're about to hear from your child will be new, exciting, and may possibly contradict everything you believe to be true in this world. Proceed with caution. Suppress emotion. Breathe deeply, and take it one gem at a time.

You may learn:

- Who they really have a crush on.
- How much homework they really have.
- The grade they really got on the math test.
- The grade everyone else really got on the math test
- What they are really posting on TikTok.
- What really happened to their backpack.
- What they really do with their lunch money.

Driving + Carpools 69

Level 2: Perspective

With enough practice, one day you will gain access to the life force energy flowing from the back seat and find a path into conversations you're not even a part of. This is your opportunity to advance beyond your individual experience to a deeper level of awareness—other parents.

You may learn:

- Which parents bring the best snacks.
- Which parents smell funny.
- Which parents call the coach all the time.
- Which parents are more uptight than you are.
- Which parents gossip more than you do.
- Which parents nag more than you do.
- Which parents are fighting.
- Which parents coach from the driver's seat.

Level 3: Transcendence

Congratulations. You have reached the highest level of human consciousness and, simultaneously, the lowest level of self-respect. Getting the goods without even being present is a feat of clever parenting and a weighty responsibility. Your station in life changes the day your child brings you an update after riding in someone else's car.

You may learn:

- Which parent texts while they drive.
- Which parent doesn't know how to drive.
- Which parent drops f-bombs.
- Which parent tries too hard.
- Which parent cares more about the game than their kid.
- Which parent says the quiet part out loud.
- Which parent is in trouble at work.
- Which parent wasn't really on a business trip.

Carpool Trust Fall

You are far enough along the parenting continuum right now to appreciate the fact that nothing is about you anymore. Ever. Maybe you've even found peace with the fact that, for the foreseeable future, me-time doesn't exist outside your bathroom, and frankly, sometimes not even inside it. For Soccer Parents, bio breaks take place in porta johns and gas station restrooms—the kind where you have to ask the cashier for the key—and, well, if you're holding your breath and trying not to let your eyes focus on anything, let's just say it may not be the respite you need.

While I can't magic you into a spa weekend or a luxury mountain retreat, I can channel the power of the carpool to give you an hour to yourself and that's practically the same thing. Even better, it's a powerful team-building exercise for the parents on your kid's team. Who needs an escape room when you can do a Carpool Trust Fall?

Required tools: Team app or whatever communication channel your team relies on.
Level of difficulty: Easy.
Timing: Can be executed at any game.

Step-by-Step Instructions

1. Drop your kid off at the next game and drive to your favorite coffee shop.
2. Post a comment in the team app that an emergency came up and your kid needs a ride home after the game.
3. Sit back, sip your drink, and watch the other parents take over.

Driving + Carpools

Expected Outcomes

Nervousness: Upon seeing your text, the other parents will a) turn to each other to wonder what horrible situation is keeping you from the game, b) reflect internally about how they'd react if they were in your shoes, and c) brainstorm excuses as to why they can't bring your kid home. From your cozy chair in the corner of the coffee shop, you'll be inspired by this moment of connection, vulnerability, and creativity.

Trust: The team admin will jump in with a note of solidarity, explaining how everyone is thinking good thoughts and hoping everything is okay, and can anybody else help you out during this tough time because she has to pull her own kid early to head to an out-of-town funeral? A few more parents will chime in with their own inventive apologies, but pretty soon regrets will change to ideas—hey, doesn't Andre live near you? Isn't your place on the way to both Marcus and Victor's neighborhoods? And there it is, authentic team-building happening on the screen in front of you—while you sip your quad-shot caramel macchiato, with vanilla syrup, two pumps of butterscotch, whipped cream, and chocolate curls.

SURVIVING SOCCER

Triumph: And then it happens. Anwar's dad, who unfortunately can't drive your son home himself, has found Victor's dad down at the playground where he was busy entertaining his two younger kids, and secured his commitment to take your child home after the game. Right before your eyes—and right next to the paperback you're finally finishing—your phone screen displays the formation of brand new communication pathways.

Bonding: Applause emojis and all manner of "Go team!" GIFs flood the team chat. It's not even halftime, but the parents have come together, faced their fears, solved a challenge, and emerged from the experience as a solid unit. Seeds of positivity and camaraderie have taken root, and you still have enough time to finish your muffin, return your book to the library, and come up with a good story to tell Victor's dad when he drops your kid off.

Empowerment: With this major win on display before them, your team's parents are recharged and ready for anything. And now you know how to give yourself an hour of me-time.

Driving + Carpools

CALCULATE YOUR AGE IN CARPOOL YEARS

Your child just started playing soccer and you don't want to miss a single second of this experience, or mar it by schlepping around some kid you don't know.	Your age minus 5.
You drive a carpool with kids who don't know each other well, so you spend the whole ride asking them questions about school and their favorite video game because you want them to feel comfortable.	Your age plus 10.
Your child doesn't like these kids and sighs loudly each time you ask one of them a question.	Your age plus 15.
Your carpool includes kids who are best buddies and have so much fun in the car that you spend the drive trying to join their conversation but are constantly ignored.	Your age plus your average weekly number of therapy sessions.

SURVIVING SOCCER

One of the kids in your carpool always takes his cleats and socks off on the ride home.	Your age plus a migraine.
You want the kids in your carpool to think you are cool so you go through the drive-thru after practice and swear them to secrecy.	Your age minus 10.
One of the kids in your carpool always calls you Mr./Mrs.—— and thanks you each time you pick them up or drop them off.	Your age plus a good night's sleep.
Your teenager is learning to drive, so you can't carpool and you have to ride to and from every practice in the passenger seat, praying for your life while they tell you you're overreacting.	Your age plus an IRS audit, sciatica, and pipes that burst while you're at an out-of-town tournament.

Driving + Carpools

Build a Better Carpool
5 Rules for Success

Getting the goods on your kid is just the beginning. Getting the system working in your favor will change your life. Enjoy dreaming about the things you should be doing with your newfound free time—even though you lose your excuse for leaving work early, not working out, and grabbing dinner in the drive-thru. Just follow these rules so you don't screw it up.

1. PRIORITIZE COMPATIBILITY

Punctuality is dogma. Choose carpool partners with a timing philosophy that matches yours. Early people, you know who you are. Stick together. It's easy to assume the most important factor is a short drive, but being compatible is essential. Even if it makes the drive longer. And even though another teammate lives three doors down, if it's a get-there-in-the-nick-of-time family or, worse, a we'll-get-there-when-we-get-there family, you are better off without them. Personality trumps geography. Trust me. Andrew may live 15 minutes from you in the opposite direction of where you're going, but when his mom texts to say she's picking up your kid 30 minutes early today because Waze notified her of potential closures and heavier traffic this evening due to a water main break, you'll know you've found your tribe.

2. LOOK FOR LARGER FAMILIES

Carpooling is the first language of families with more kids than drivers. They're generous in helping you achieve fluency because it's in their best interest. Since they're always at someone's practice, game, rehearsal, or recital, they don't do phone calls and are great

SURVIVING SOCCER

texters, which makes it easier to ignore their comments about how complicated their lives are. Also, they're quick to suggest a carpool schedule and flexible enough to change it when you need to. They know the best meet-up spots, and they've always got an extra of whatever your kid forgot.

3. EMBRACE DIVORCE

More households = more drivers. Don't miss an opportunity to let another family's misfortune make your life easier. Not just any divorce, either. Look for hostile split-custody situations. If each half of the divorced couple acts like a separate piece of the carpool puzzle in a two-kid carpool, you'll be dividing shifts by three. Add another kid or two and you can take a vacation. You're welcome.

4. KEEP QUIET

Besides an over-the-top welcome and a hearty see-ya-later when kids (other than yours) enter and exit your vehicle, your audio level should be zero. Don't sing with the radio. Don't sing without the radio. Don't talk to yourself. Don't talk to the asshole who nearly ran your car off the road. Don't use your horn. Don't ask your child about school or friends, and especially not about practice. Don't ask the other kids about the video they're all laughing at on their phones. Don't burp or fart (audibly). Don't listen to political radio shows, and don't forget to disconnect the Bluetooth of the sexy audiobook you've been listening to in the car while they're at practice.

5. TAKE RESPONSIBILITY

What they don't tell you about driving the carpool is that it has little to do with driving. During your shift, you are unwittingly

Driving + Carpools

committed to be the parent-like person for each child you transport. That's before, during, and after practice. Make sure you're willing to do this job with each child, even the one who talks about how much money his parents have and how he doesn't have a bedtime. You'll recognize him by the $300 cleats he'll outgrow before the end of the season. Injuries, forgotten water bottles, and any form that the admin insists needs to be signed are yours to deal with. This should be obvious, but practice forging the other parents' signatures.

Parking Lot Time Maximizers

Not sure what to do while you wait out the practice clock on the nights you drive? You've got plenty of options:

- Watch practice so you are prepared to provide your child with specific feedback on his performance on the way home.
- Exercise in full view of the team, wearing workout clothes you should have retired years ago and probably should have never purchased in the first place.
- Read a trashy book in your car so everyone thinks you're smart and no one can see the cover or is close enough to ask what you're reading.
- Chat with other parents about how often the coach calls you to talk about how talented your child is.
- Relax in your car with the engine running for the whole 90 minutes of practice while all the other cars are off with their windows open to enjoy the breeze.
- Play the radio in your car loud enough that everyone can hear it even if their windows are up.

- Call Great Uncle Gus, your mom, housecleaner, travel agent, neighbor, and BFF on speaker phone.
- Be social with parents you don't know very well by inviting them to happy hour during practice.
- Run errands and underestimate lines and traffic so that when you get back, practice is long over and the admin is waiting in a dark, empty parking lot with your kid.
- Share your thoughts with parents you don't know about how the coach is tanking the season by giving certain players more time on the field than they deserve.
- Work in your mobile office and tell everyone who walks by how important your job is.
- Introduce yourself to parents you don't know by asking them to drive your child to the out-of-state games this weekend because you are finally getting that weekend away you deserve.

Driving + Carpools

PART III

GET YOUR GAME ON

CHAPTER 7

Packing + Planning

*If you don't have at least three types of blankets in your trunk,
are you even a Soccer Parent?*

Please pat yourself on the back for getting your kid to the right soccer field at the right time with the right gear. This is a thing and you have just done this thing, so please recognize yourself. No one else will.

However, you are not a Soccer Parent success story yet. Your child's future on the field is not some pot roast you put in a slow-cooker and can forget about all day. It's more of a temperamental risotto that must be constantly watched and stirred.

Don't Forget the Shower Caddy

The Ultimate Packing List

Your biggest preseason responsibility—next to jockeying the family calendar—is getting yourself game ready. No matter how independent your child is, in the last five to 50 minutes before you're supposed to leave for the game, they will ambush you. Your ultimate worth as a human being will be swiftly and mercilessly measured by your ability to instantaneously locate their shin guards, headphones, black socks, black-striped socks (*no*, the other black-striped socks), good jersey, math homework, water bottle, other water bottle, favorite shorts, phone charger, muscle tape, or lucky headband.

Now, the fact that you've gotten this far tells me your organizational skills are already unrivaled in the county or at least among the parents of your kid's classmates. Nevertheless, you're going to need to ratchet it up to DEFCON 1 on game days. We're talking maximum readiness. This means your stuff gets packed the night before.

Seating

Forget about comfort, your butt, and whether or not you can even feel it at the end of the game. You will quickly learn that the best chair is the one that's easiest to carry. You will spend more time holding your chair than you ever held your newborn. Pick one you can lug through gravel parking lots, classroom nature preserves, unfamiliar school campuses (the long way), between sidelines, and through shoe-obliterating muddy fields. Where, finally, you'll stand for a half-hour waiting for the game before your kid's game to end, and for those parents to finish socializing, pack up everything they own, and move on before you can set your chair down. You'll be too anxious to sit by then anyway.

Weather Gear

The smart move is to keep rain, wind, sun, heat, cold, and snow protection in your car year-round. You're going to want options. Example: not all blankets are equal. First you've got your fleece, the social butterfly of blankets. You may not realize it, but you have eight to 10 of these suckers floating around your house. Recognize them by their garish, clip-art designs: soccer balls, cartoon dogs, rainbows, ballerina slippers, superheroes, or the logo of a sports team someone in your family liked for five minutes. They will be plentiful, based on the number of kids you have multiplied by the number of gift-bearing-but-don't-know-you-that-well relatives in your circle. Sadly, fleece blankets are only effective for mild temps and wind speeds.

Then there's your old bedspread. The workhorse. It's been with you forever and done its job for years in silent resignation. Once the *pièce de résistance* of your bedroom, it's fallen down the ladder of usefulness, hitting a few rungs on the way—guest room covering, winter topper, camping quilt—and has now assumed its career-closing role as a trunk blanket. No one will notice the rips and dog stains, plus it's big enough to cover you and your spouse. This alleviates some of the tension when said spouse realizes you packed weather gear only for yourself.

Of course, you'll also want to have the Swiss Army Knife of protection, the stadium blanket. Warm on one side, waterproof on the other, and large enough to cover you plus one. Honestly, though, you'll be a lot more comfortable if you hog the whole thing and swaddle yourself in it. For the money, this heavy-hitter should park the car, make hot cocoa, and rub your feet too.

This is how you need to approach all your weather gear. For hats, sunglasses, and umbrellas, jackets and coats, boots, scarves, gloves, and mittens. Think options, range, and backups. Plus, the more of these items you can find in your team's colors, the less of a jinx you'll be. Also, multiples. An extra umbrella to offer up to another parent in a downpour or a pair of shades to give out in the blinding sun earn you GET OUT OF JAIL FREE cards for the rest of the season. I'm talking carpool shifts, snack rotations, and even your $\frac{1}{16}^{th}$ portion of the coach's end-of-year gift.

Extra points if all your gear fits into a team-colored tote or wagon that you lug—along with that chair—to the field for every game *just in case*. Remember, once you get to the field, your survival depends on how well you planned and packed. It doesn't matter if you're five minutes or five hours from home, when you're at the field you're on your own. If the weather doesn't go as planned, you're basically stranded in the *Apollo 13* solving scene—without the geniuses at NASA frantically trying to help you fit a square peg into a round hole. Your best bet is to bring the whole coat closet with you.

Beverages

If you're not ready to put your Diet Coke problem on full display, drink from a trendy stainless steel water bottle so people know you're saving the planet. Practice your deep-breathing and mindfulness visualization techniques for the parents who bring those loud, crinkly, by-the-carload-sized cases of bottled water that they squeeze and twist with their game-time anxiety.

One more thing. We need to have a serious talk about drinking at games. You know your body best. Only you know what you can truly handle. Just remember, there is a fine line between minimal hydration and the maximum distance to the nearest porta john. Don't say I didn't warn you.

Sustenance

Pre-wrapped meal replacement/protein/energy/snack bars are the easiest way to deal with hunger, but a reusable container full of organic carrot sticks shows everyone you're there to win. Only amateurs buy a bag of baby carrots.

If you're coming to the game straight from work, your other kid's game, the airport, the gym, the DMV, church, your therapist's office, your attorney's office, a wedding (and you skipped the reception), or funeral (same), then feel free to share this excuse loudly as you unwrap whatever fast food you "grabbed on the way" because you were "dying of hunger." Maybe don't say "dying" if you're post-funeral. Just know that you'll be subject to the stares of everyone who can't believe you eat that garbage and everyone else who can't get over how good it smells.

Entertainment

I've got news. Soccer games aren't all soccer. Two 30-minute halves are, in full, a two-hour affair. Minimum. You've got pregame warm-ups, halftime, and the coach's 20-minute postgame debriefing. Lots of downtime. Think about how you want to play it. Are you going to be comfortable engaging with others or do you need a prop? Plan accordingly.

Phones make an easy go-to—*if they are charged*. You could play a game, but do you really want everyone to know you like Kwazy Cupcakes?

Packing + Planning

Also, social media is a trap. Other parents could ask to follow you, and it's either going to be 1) the gossipy one who wants to see the pics you post from inside your house so she can tell everyone how you live; 2) the competitive one who wants to fill your feed with all the amazing things her kids do; 3) the insecure one who thinks that once you see all the posts of her workout stats you'll finally decide to be friends with her irl, even though she sits by herself and never speaks to anyone; or 4) the one who's already made five passive-aggressive posts about the game you're in the middle of watching. Plus, people will assume you can talk and scroll at the same time and may engage with you anyway.

What you really need is the mother of all conversation stoppers: a book. You get to sit quietly, looking and feeling peaceful, under an impenetrable force field of "Leave me the F alone." Level up with an e-reader. Have fun making up highly intellectual or wildly inappropriate titles when another parent asks you what you're reading in a tone that suggests you're being antisocial. (Even if it's the mom who's a cop and reminds everyone that she carries 24/7.)

Miscellaneous Essentials

Learning from your own experience is overrated. Better to gain from those of us who came before you and avoid traumatic situations in the first place by keeping these things on hand. This is only a partial list, but it will get you started. Tweezers, wet wipes, eye drops, moisturizer, bug spray, $40 in small bills, a portable battery charger, resealable plastic bags, cotton balls, a glue stick, used coffee grounds, a penlight, hand sanitizer, dry shampoo, headphones, highlighters, electrical tape, adhesive bandages, packets of mustard, hair bands, and deodorant. I can't tell you how or when or where you'll need these things, but trust me, at some point you'll thank me.

If You Read Nothing Else

If you don't get this one part right, you can forget about the rest. Lateness is your kryptonite. The later your kid is, the weaker he looks to the coach. Long-term exposure is deadly.

GET.

YOUR KID.

TO THE GAME.

ON TIME.

Thanks to the hard work of your team admin and the wonders of technology, you'll get notifications for all team events on every electronic device you own. But, assuming you're not an expert in the personal settings of the latest OS, expect to get these reminders 15 minutes before the game is about to start.

Now, if you remember nothing else, remember this. Fifteen minutes is just enough time to process the fact that you have failed your child, and their soccer career is over before it started. Set. Your. Own. Alerts.

As a courtesy, below is a sample alarm schedule.

Sample Alarm Schedule for Parents Who Love Their Kids

24 Hours Pre-Kickoff

- Fill car with gas.
- Verify game location and address.
- Map it.
- Check satellite view.
- Notice neighboring wildlife sanctuary on map and recall runaway donkey incident the last time you played there.

Packing + Planning

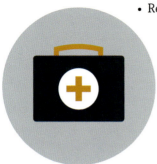

- Restock first-aid kit.
- Note size of parking lot and gauge lot-to-field walk time.
- Get total travel-time estimate.
- Double travel time to include buffer for returning home for forgotten cleats.
- Worry about whether her cleats still fit her.
- Google hours for sporting goods store to see if it's too late to get new cleats.
- Calculate departure time.
- Locate the three closest coffee shops to the field.

Six Hours Pre-Kickoff

- Triple-check gas tank.
- Swing by mechanic to double-check gas gauge is working.
- Check forecast on phone app for potential weather-related driving delays.
- Compare reviews and download six more weather apps to confirm forecast.
- Bake a coffee cake for your neighbor and lose an hour asking if her achy knees sense a rainstorm.
- Try to remember if your sump pump is more than 10 years old and what you stand to lose if your basement floods while you're at the game.
- Spend an hour in the basement looking for your middle-school

SURVIVING SOCCER

scrapbooks to make sure they're not in boxes on the floor, should there be a flood.
- Recalculate drive-time estimate.
- Readjust departure time if necessary.

Three Hours Pre-Kickoff

- Launch your two favorite navigation apps and analyze minimum three routes to your destination on each app.

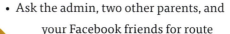

- Ask the admin, two other parents, and your Facebook friends for route recommendations.
- Start taking long, deep, cleansing breaths.
- Search your digital calendar to find out if you already have a checkup with your doctor scheduled in the next six months and ponder whether you would have time to get in later this week if you told them about your stress headaches.
- Finalize departure time.
- Tell everyone riding with you when you expect them to be in the car ready to go.
- Begin obsessing over what you're going to have for dinner after the game.
- Google how long cooked rice lasts in the fridge.

One Hour Pre-Departure

- Check local news for incidents of overturned semis spilling paint, wine, or thousands of pounds of sausage across the freeway.

- Settle on a route.
- Refresh app to make sure you have the correct travel time for that route.
- Refresh app again.
- Remember that you told your boss you'd finish up and send a report to him in 10 minutes, three hours ago.
- Re-confirm timing with everyone who is riding in your car.
- Refresh app again.

30 Minutes Pre-Departure

- Start screaming.

Long after you've dropped your kid at the field for warm-ups, while you're waiting to place your coffee order inside a café two miles from the park, the team app's 15-minute alert will tell you exactly when it's time to lie your way to the front of the line so you can get your latte and not miss kickoff.

What Doesn't Kill You
A Playlist for Packing
Packing for your night of driving the carpool requires some forethought. Packing for a Saturday game takes a list, an Advil, and a moment to think about your life choices. And the only thing that will get you through the experience of packing for an out-of-town tournament weekend—assuming your therapist isn't willing to be on call all night—is the right playlist.

SURVIVING SOCCER

"Good Feeling" by Flo Rida	You walk into your kid's room to tell her to start packing, and her whole uniform is neatly arranged—including both jerseys and three pairs of field socks—on her bed.
"Breathe" by Anna Nalick	You open the water bottle cabinet in your kitchen to get your favorite travel tumbler—the one with triple-wall insulation that you splurged on for your birthday—but it's not there.
"I'm So Excited" by The Pointer Sisters	You confirm that your soccer-parent bestie is attending and bringing the XBox, so your kids can hang out in their room between games while you two hide from the other parents in yours.
"What's Going On?" by Marvin Gaye	You crawl through your car looking for your tumbler and find fast-food wrappers, empty Gatorade bottles, a warm-up jacket you've never seen before, and a page from someone named Kyle's math homework with a muddy cleat print across it. But no tumbler.

Packing + Planning

"Let It Be" by The Beatles	From the trunk of your car, you hear your dog throwing up inside the house.
"The Climb" by Miley Cyrus	You get a team app notification that your second game was rescheduled for three hours after the first, at a field two hours away from it.
"Blessed" by Elton John	You pass the flier on the fridge for the school's dress-like-your-favorite-meme fundraiser, which is this weekend—while you're in Canton, Ohio, for the tournament.
"I Will Survive" by Gloria Gaynor	You check the weekend forecast, which includes heavy rain, dangerous winds, and a potential for flurries. You remember how the triple-wall insulation of your missing tumbler keeps coffee deliciously lava-hot for 16 hours.
"Shake It Off" by Taylor Swift	You realize that you didn't let the canopy dry out before you packed it up last weekend.

"Trouble" by Dave Matthews	Your kid says she can't find her lucky headband—the one she won't let you wash and that the dog often digs out of her soccer bag.
"Beautiful Day" by U2	You clean and pack the fresh fruit and veggies you bought for the trip.
"Celebration" by Kool & the Gang	You remember to pack a stash of hand warmers.
"Happy" by Pharrell Williams	You remember that pot is legal in Ohio and pack your actual stash.
"Lose Yourself" by Eminem	Your kid tells you that her science fair project is due on Monday and she hasn't started it yet, and could you help her figure out how to turn on a lightbulb with a potato.
"Don't Give Up" by Peter Gabriel	You walk into the living room where you've carefully laid out everything that needs to be packed and find dog vomit and bits of the lucky headband everywhere.

Packing + Planning

"On Top of the World" by Imagine Dragons	You pat yourself on the back for filling up the gas tank yesterday.
"Waiting on the World to Change" by John Mayer	Your kid throws her soccer bag down the stairs and when it hits the bottom step, everything falls out, including your travel tumbler, which she has stuffed with the gel packs she uses on her feet between games.
"Survivor" by Destiny's Child	You fit everything into the car and can still see out through the rearview mirror.
"Life Is a Highway" by Tom Cochran	You drive away from your house, realizing you never cleaned the dog vomit off the couch.

WHAT YOUR ARRIVAL TIME SAYS ABOUT YOUR VALUE AS A HUMAN

Do not make the rookie mistake of putting the game time on your calendar. We've all done it, and we all still remember—years later—the look on everyone's faces when we innocently strolled up to the field at 10-till, thinking we were a few glorious minutes early only to see their pity and then watch our kid sit out the first half of the game.

Unlike a work meeting, game time is not when you casually start heading to the designated location, stopping for a bio break, a bit of gossip, or to

SURVIVING SOCCER

dip into the candy bowl on Becky's desk. Game time is when all the players are completely dressed in their uniforms, shoes tied, warmed up, in position on the field. The referee blows the kickoff whistle at game time. When, exactly, your kid needs to arrive at the field, is up to your coach.

This is one of those few reasons for which you should attempt a direct conversation with the coach. You need to know his timing expectations. Do it early in the season, do it quickly, and do it with deference. I'm not saying he won't still act annoyed—that's pretty much his job—but you and every other parent within earshot will enjoy the benefit of a lower, more stable blood pressure once you know exactly how many minutes before kickoff the coach wants your kid at the field. Now, whatever number he tells you, add 20.

Not convinced? Let's play it out then. Besides, there is a sliding scale of shame depending on precisely how late you get your kid to the field. We'll start with the most heinous—and yet most common—then work our way backward into the coach's good graces:

Show up at kickoff—All the other parents will watch your kid, with his ginormous soccer backpack bouncing over his shoulder, run awkwardly around the field to the team bench where he will sit for the entire first half. Silver lining: you will miss this spectacle because the closest parking spot is three miles away. Don't worry, though, at least one parent will enjoy telling you all about it when you arrive at halftime.

Get there partway through the pregame warm-up—Watch as your kid sits alone with all the other kids' backpacks while he gets his shin guards and cleats on. Cue the teasing from his buddies on the field. Expect the coach to loudly designate your kid as the one who has to gather up all the cones, balls, and any other equipment before the game starts.

Arrive at the start of the pregame warm-up—Your kid joins the only two of his teammates still getting ready, the ones whose stalling ability rivals your spouse's when it's time to go to your parents' for dinner. Expect the coach's joke about whether or not your kid can tell time.

Packing + Planning

Step onto the field 10 minutes before warm-ups—Your kid joins a quickly growing pack of teammates engaged in a lively conversation with topics that include:

- Bodily functions
- Pop quizzes
- Video games
- Hair
- Bruises in strange places
- Pizza
- Chafing
- Cellphone battery levels
- Icing groin injuries
- Mystery smells

Pull into the lot 30-plus minutes before warm-ups—You beat everyone to the field, even the coach. You earned not just a minute to breathe and to think about that coffee you now have time to go get once your kid bails out of the car, you've also earned a gold star for the day.

Spelled out like this, it seems simple. Don't be fooled. It's gonna take you a while to train your brain. Even for you early people. Getting to the field at the right time is not as easy as it looks. Don't be surprised if you finally get it down right about the time your child is old enough to drive himself to warm-ups and you can finally start paying attention to game time.

WARNING—At some point, another parent is going to offer to take your kid to a game. Listen to me. Take a beat. Think it through. It doesn't matter how badly you could use that time, how much you can taste those extra minutes, which you will inevitably spend emptying the dishwasher. Do not agree to this proposition until you are certain that this parent has a firm understanding of arrival times and when you expect your child to be delivered to the field.

Soccer Parenting and Nutrition

The more soccer your child plays, the more you're going to think about nutrition. You may ask yourself what foods will fuel her growing body and give her the energy she needs to perform her best on the field. Just don't ask Facebook. That's a rabbit-hole-sized comment thread you will not come back from the same. You'll see terms like "meal prepping," "energy balls," and "fresh vegetables." You'll see photos of fridges lined with perfectly portioned packets of boiled chicken breasts, neatly tied bundles of match-sticked carrots, mounds of mouthwatering oranges, peeled and sectioned. Before you beat yourself up over the bagel bites you nuked for your kid at 10:00 PM last night, remember that AI-generated images are free and easy to come by, and if any of those folks really did prepare such fancy-schmancy meals for their kids, they wouldn't have time for social media.

The quicker you familiarize yourself with the real food options you'll have to choose from during your child's soccer career, the easier meal planning will be.

Packing + Planning

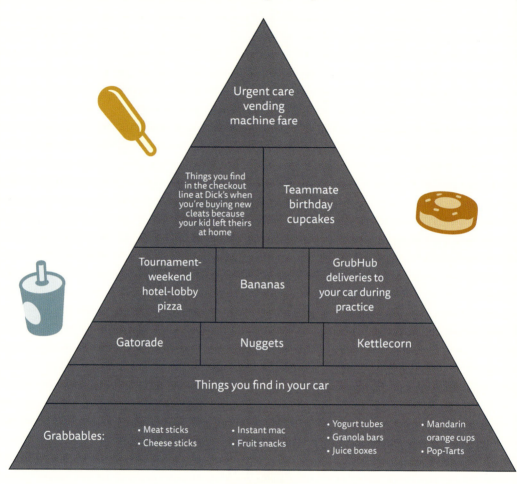

Soccer Parenting Food Pyramid

- Urgent care vending machine fare
- Things you find in the checkout line at Dick's when you're buying new cleats because your kid left theirs at home
- Teammate birthday cupcakes
- Tournament-weekend hotel-lobby pizza
- Bananas
- GrubHub deliveries to your car during practice
- Gatorade
- Nuggets
- Kettlecorn
- Things you find in your car
- Grabbables:
  - Meat sticks
  - Cheese sticks
  - Instant mac
  - Fruit snacks
  - Yogurt tubes
  - Granola bars
  - Juice boxes
  - Mandarin orange cups
  - Pop-Tarts

SURVIVING SOCCER

CHAPTER 8

Sideline Strategy

Welcome back to your middle-school cafeteria.
Be careful where you sit.

Where you sit at your kid's soccer game is a delicate and complex decision. Choose wisely.

Know before you go:

1. Spectators are expected to stay on the half of the sideline that is opposite their team's bench.
2. Sitting on the "wrong" half of the sideline is a surefire way to distract the other team's fans by provoking uncontrollable anger.
3. No one has ever successfully enforced this rule.

Who's Who? A Sideline Manifesto

The Zealots

The perfect spot for the most committed, engaged, rule-following Soccer Parent is a hair's breadth from midfield, as close to the center line as you can get and still be on your team's side. All the action—including not just the play of game, but referee disputes, and whatever is going on with the other team's parents—will never be very far, even after halftime when the players switch sides. Also, by sitting in the spot that is closest to the opponent's side, you are the de facto representative of your team. The responsibilities of this role come into play when the other team's spectators yell at your players, make fun of your coach, or accuse the ref of being biased toward your team.

The In-Crowd
Parking your chair five to 20 feet from midfield guarantees you will be at the center of the game's social activity. This is what a 12-year-old would call "the cool kids' table." Whether they like you or not, other parents will set their chairs next to yours because it's prime real estate—close to the action but with a one-family (*see* "The Zealots") buffer from the opposing side's fans. This is your chance to finally be part of the popular group, or at least look like it.

The Socially Distanced
Provided you remembered your prescription sunglasses, you really can see well no matter where you sit. And if you're a no-drama llama, the farther you are from the parental action—your team's and the other side's—the better. Even though you won't be the only one seeking out this inconspicuously valuable real estate, the others will keep at least a chair's width of distance, if not more.

The Keeper's Parents
This isn't a real spot unless your child is a goalkeeper, in which case you'll want to be as close as you can get to the goal box. Following the logic that people do well under pressure, why not add more by being in

SURVIVING SOCCER

your kid's peripheral vision as a competitor sprints down the field and attempts to kick the soccer ball as hard as they can at them?

The Standers & Pacers

The pressure of these games can get to a person. And you can only yell so loud. For some parents, the next step, often an involuntary reaction, is physical movement. Stand or pace behind the row of chairs, and you'll release some steam and hit your steps goal for the day.

The Self-Exiled

For some, the excitement of the game truly is just too much. Maybe your kid is set to take a penalty kick that could win the game for the team. Maybe your team is down by more points than they've scored all season. Or maybe the wind chill is below zero. This is when you "watch" from your car. Bribe the admin into texting you highlights and your kid may never know the difference.

Spies & Double Agents

While it is true that you are supposed to stay on your half of the sideline (meaning, directly across from your team's bench), even when the players switch halves, some parents self-select out of this "rule" because nothing gets in the way of, well, their doing whatever they want. If you too possess this type of...commitment...you can look forward to learning what the other teams' parents think of their coach, your coach, and your kid when they take one of their kids down. And when one of them politely asks you to sit on your team's side, do give them a lesson in how "It's just a game," and, "They're just kids," and how they should "grow up and act like an adult," right after your kid's team scores on theirs and you scream, *"That's what you get, suckers!"* in their ears.

ANATOMY OF A SOCCER SIDELINE

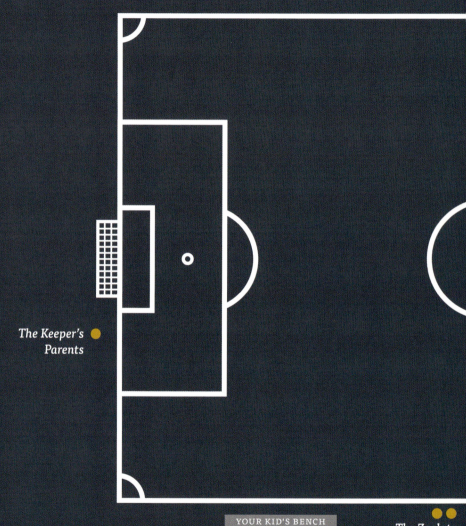

The Keeper's Parents

YOUR KID'S BENCH

The Zealots

The Standers & Pacers

The In-Crowd

The Socially Distanced

SURVIVING SOCCER

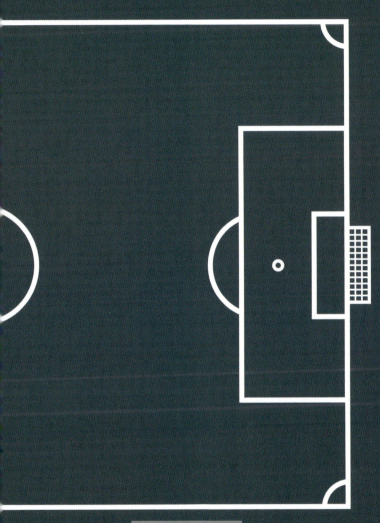

OTHER TEAM'S BENCH

● ● Spies & Double Agents

The Self-Exiled

Sideline Strategy 105

Diagram Your Sideline Conversation

Just like every subculture, youth soccer has its own lexicon. Parents may wield it like a secret handshake for an exclusive club they're waiting to decide if you can belong to, but the truth is, not all of it matters. Some of it you can ignore. For example, whether you call them cleats, boots, or soccer shoes, they will still cost more than any pair of shoes you have ever bought yourself. Some of it you can just pretend to know. If you keep your mouth shut, you can make it all the way to your child's Senior Night soccer game without really understanding the offside rule. But some of it—the casual banter between parents on the sideline—you're going to want to understand, because Soccer Parents play to win, and not just on the field.

Forget flashcards, this is all about context. Let's diagram some examples:

> **Situation:** *You've just congratulated Joseph's mom for the beautiful goal he scored moments ago, while your child still sits on the bench, hoping to be subbed in at some point during the game.*

Joseph's mom: That's <u>so kind of you, but honestly</u>, it's about time he woke up and started actually playing. I don't know what's gotten into him lately, but <u>he just isn't playing his best</u>. Maybe it's <u>exhaustion from all the extra practices with the Academy team</u>? I was <u>just telling Coach Tom last night</u>—we

> You clearly don't know anything about soccer.

> I have a higher standard of excellence than you do, and it shows.

> I didn't want to tell you, but I want you to know my child is special.

> I have the coach wrapped around my finger.

told him to <u>come enjoy our pool any time</u> he wants since he's always so busy during the day with our boys, that poor man— that I don't care that the Academy director thinks Joseph is the <u>best player he's seen</u> <u>come through the system</u>, our kid <u>made</u> <u>a commitment to this club team and he's</u> <u>going to keep it</u>. If that means the Academy team has to wait a year, so be it. <u>You know?</u>

> There is no depth we won't sink to if it means getting more time with the coach. And it's even better if he feels he owes us.

> Remember, my kid is better than your kid. Like, way better.

> We plan on ditching this pansy-ass team like a half-empty bottle of warm Gatorade.

> Wow, isn't it sad that your child isn't good enough to have such problems?

Situation: *You've just confessed to Taylor's mom your fear that your Abigail isn't going to get much playing time today since she had to sit out a few games after breaking her arm playing in the pool with her friends.*

Taylor's mom: Oh, of course Coach Greg will put Abigail in! <u>I know for a fact</u> that she is one of his favorites! I'm so glad she's able to play again. <u>Gosh, we</u> <u>missed her so much</u> in the big game against United. <u>I just can't believe</u> <u>we won without her</u>.

> I want you to think I have lots of private conversations with the coach and he tells me all about the other players. He does not.

> What a relief it was not to have to worry we'd get scored on each time your child was subbed in.

> Thank goodness she was not cleared to play by her doctor or we never would have won.

Sideline Strategy

He only put Missy in Abigail's spot until Abigail gets her confidence back. I know if I let Taylor be that reckless—swimming pools really are just accidents waiting to happen—she'd have broken both her arms! That's also why she eats so many leafy greens. She knows they're full of calcium, and if she wants to keep advancing her game—and move on to better teams—she needs strong bones.

> put Missy in Abigail's spot → Missy is much better than Abigail.
>
> if I let Taylor be that reckless → Where'd you learn how to parent? Off the back of a cereal box?
>
> she eats so many leafy greens → I am a very good parent.
>
> She knows they're full of calcium → I remind my kid that I am a very good parent.
>
> better teams → I can't wait until we can move on to a team where the other kids are as good as mine.

Situation: *You've just thanked Kell's parents for hosting the team potluck at their home after the final game of the season.*

Kell's dad: We're happy to do it. Honestly, this experience has been so great for Kell that we love opportunities like this where we can support the team and give back. That's why my company wanted to be the sole jersey sponsor. We even

> this experience has been so great for Kell → Your kid is very lucky to be on a team with our kid.
>
> we can support the team and give back → I believe that if I do more for the team, my child will be a better player. So far, so good.
>
> my company wanted to be the sole jersey sponsor → I'd like every parent on the team to understand how committed I am to my child being the best, and also that I have more money than you.

SURVIVING SOCCER

pay for Coach Ben's family to have an

> We will stop at nothing to be the coach's favorites. And we have more money than you.

extra room on tournament weekends—

just don't tell anyone else, that's kind of

> Tell everyone you know.

on the down-low!

> I'd like every parent to know this by the end of practice.

Kell's mom: Your Sanjay sure played

> I'm so surprised your kid didn't screw up again!

well in the game today! Did you put

> There's no way your kid suddenly got good.

Red Bull in his water bottle? I'm so glad

he finally found his confidence this

> What a shame he didn't start to play well until the last game of the season. I'm going to pretend that your kid is a decent player and just lacks confidence.

season. Listen, any time Sanjay wants

to spend some extra time on the ball,

just drop him off here. Kell is always out

> Your child really needs to practice more. Like, a lot more.

back kicking the ball, conditioning, or

> We trained our child to be self-driven, which is why he is so exceptional.

scrimmaging with whoever is around.

> I'd be happy to let our child hone his skills by running your child into the ground.

Sideline Strategy

21 PEOPLE TO AVOID AT THE GAME

- Either parent of the kid who doesn't like yours
- Either parent of the kid your kid "accidentally" injured at practice
- The mom who really wants you to join her book club
- The couple who really wants you to join their Bible study
- The dad who played soccer in college
- The mom who is always looking for volunteers to help coordinate group activities for the kids
- The coach's girlfriend
- The coach's mom
- The coach's mom's girlfriend
- The dad who brings lots of work folders and papers that he shuffles around during the game
- The couple that sits together but is always in a fight
- The dad who wishes his kid was playing football instead
- The mom who thinks this is all a massive waste of time and money
- The grandpa who calls all the (fill-in-the-stereotype) kids by the same name
- The group of younger siblings trying to recruit an adult to take them to the snack bar
- The dad who likes to tell everyone how shitty his kid is playing

SURVIVING SOCCER

- The couple who thinks you'll just love their time-share
- The mom who always wants to talk about Our Lord and Savior Jesus Christ
- Any adult with their kid's team name or colors painted on their face
- The family that brings three young kids, a dog, a grandparent, two iPads, a case of juice boxes, and a person-sized bag of kettle corn
- The cool couple who is super-friendly, but whose names you can never remember

Sideline Like a Pro

1. Start with a universal ice-breaker, e.g., traffic, weather, your marriage problems, the abortion you had in high school.
2. Knowing other parents' names is not a prerequisite for conversations of any depth.
3. If you're more than two games into the season, it's too late to ask them their name, anyway.
4. Any conversation can be interrupted by the game at any point, with no need to return to it.
5. Any compromising info you share about your kid in casual conversation to the parent next to you might be used against him by their kid at a later date.

Sideline Strategy

Soccer Is Your Kid's Only Activity Worth Watching—Change My Mind

If you haven't been asked to "watch me" build a tower of blocks, knock down a tower of blocks, go down the slide, go up the slide, jump off the side of the pool, jump from the couch to the ottoman, blow a bubble, blow a bigger bubble, blow an even bigger bubble, or blow the biggest bubble in the entire universe, are you even a parent?

Nevertheless, you can't watch everything. Nor should you. Watching your kid is super-important, but the key is to find the right things to watch. Childhood is packed with supposedly sacred events that you will be told you need to see.

In truth, the only thing you really need to watch are soccer games. Here's why:

1. No school play, concert, or recognition ceremony is worth the effort it takes to find a parking spot and a seat.
2. Can you really hear your kid's voice/instrument above all the others? More importantly, can she see you in that dark, packed school auditorium?
3. Hours-long baseball games, swim meets, and dance recitals yield an excessively poor ratio of sitting through every other child's performance to your own kid's 90-second appearance. You do not get this time back at the end of your life.
4. No one loves their kid enough to watch them play video games.
5. Watching your kid eat his vegetables or take out the trash doesn't count because you're only paying attention to make sure he does it.

Game—Laugh, Worry, Kill

If you insist on embracing your whole not-judging-others vibe, then, first of all, good for you. That makes one of us. However, it is possible that when the coach sends out a text at midnight on Friday that Saturday's game is at 8:00 AM, not 3:00 PM, like the schedule says, laughter may be your safest option. Then there's the ref who you believe is either rooting for the other team to win or hasn't updated his glasses prescription in a few years. It's also entirely possible that there will come a time when you'll want to drop-kick that one parent on your team into the back of their perfectly packed SUV. That's okay. It's all okay. It's just part of the Soccer Parent experience. Laugh. Worry. Kill. Just play along.

Parent Edition

Laugh: The parent who shares their pop-up canopy and the responsibility for entertaining their three-year-old triplets during the game.
Worry: The parent who compliments your kid and has suggestions for how you can better parent them.
Kill: The parent who always offers to give your kid rides, and delivers political hot takes in the car.

Sideline Strategy

Coach Edition

Laugh: The coach who you can hear a mile away, yelling at your kid or praising him.

Worry: The coach who doesn't interrupt the players during games and doesn't talk to parents before or after them.

Kill: The coach who has a sense of humor and uses it against your kid in the middle of a game.

Ref Edition

Laugh: The ref who takes time to explain every call and remind everyone of his power.

Worry: The ref who lets the kids play and also lets the kids foul each other.

Kill: The ref who wants to be everyone's friend more than anyone's game official.

What to Do When You Hit Your (Soccer-Parenting) Limit

It happens once every season. At every age level. With every group of parents. The whistle blows to end the game. A win, thank God. The kids skip off the field with energy they didn't appear to have for the past 45 minutes. Muscle memory has you folding up your chair and digging for your keys, while your brain is rummaging around your kitchen pantry trying to figure out what could pass for dinner.

That's when you hear it: "Why don't we get the team together this weekend and do something fun?"

You're pretty sure you'd rather sign up for a colonoscopy than spend another minute listening to Kayla's dad's triathlon regimen or Sienna's mom talk about her grass allergy. And you're probably not alone. But the jubilation of the win has put beer goggles on the lot of you.

The intoxication is real. Everyone's sorry-we're-busy reflexes are dulled. The lubrication of victory has them believing that spending an additional two hours together this week is the best idea anyone has had, ever.

And so it begins.

The dad next to you, who, based on his wife's weekly testimonials, would starve to death if left on his own in the kitchen, suggests a team potluck. He generously offers to host since their pool is done and the full-size turf field they built right next to it is all set up. This will mean more time making small talk with people you already don't know what to say to, while your kids, hopped up on 3-percent-juice boxes and grocery store cookies, do cannonballs into the pool. Yeah, no.

Someone behind you suggests booking time at the new indoor skydiving park that's getting so much buzz. But all you hear is an expensive, not-the-way-you'd-spend-your-free-time activity that has a greater-than-50-percent chance of ending at urgent care. Hard pass.

Your (now former) soccer-parent bestie proposes going to an MLS match. O joy! more soccer, and this time with no one you're related to on the field. You calculate whether you have enough time to apply for a second mortgage to cover the trips to the snack bar, replica jerseys, team scarves, and $20 commemorative mini soccer balls every parent will feel compelled to buy after Victor's dad buys him one. Will they see your last-minute text claiming that you can't find parking near the stadium and sadly can't make it?

Finally, one parent (you know which one) will suggest a community service activity. But an afternoon reading books to dogs in a shelter seems awfully risky when your own pets are one soccer-practice-ran-long-again short of telling Alexa to dial the ASPCA. Zero tail wags for this one.

Sideline Strategy

So, there you stand, holding your keys, your car in sight. You are thoughtfully considering your fight-or-flight response while your kid channels Mister Rogers, changing out of her socks and cleats like she gets paid for it by the second. Maybe you can hear your therapist's voice in your head, suggesting you compliment all the great ideas and then, with honesty and maturity, let everyone know you are not interested in participating this time. Or perhaps you can't hear the dulcet tones of his voice over the Madagascar Hissing Cockroach that appears to be trapped inside your prefrontal cortex.

Either way, just remember you always have options:

- Declare that, regretfully, your weekend is already booked solid.
- Feign being sick.
- Actually get sick.
- Invent the existence of another child who already has a team activity this weekend.
- Claim car trouble.
- Claim a winning lotto ticket (*someone's* got to win).
- Claim an existential crisis.
- Dust off your intention to be more social.
- Dust off your passport.
- Commit a third-degree misdemeanor.
- Commit yourself.
- Commit to bringing your legendary Tater Tot casserole to the pool party.

CHAPTER 9

Injuries

The referee—who works in IT—will be assessing your kid's injury.

Soccer players aren't called floppers for no reason. However, for a fast-paced, full-body, and very often full-contact sport where the players' only protection is a lightweight piece of plastic that slips into the fronts of their socks, injuries do happen. No matter how much of a helicopter, snowplow, or earthmover parent you are, you can't prevent them, but you can be prepared.

Know that the moment your child goes to the ground and play is stopped, the air becomes tense with uncertainty. You will be right there and yet you will have no idea what happened to them, because you are at least 20 yards away, and when they went down you were either talking to the mom next to you, looking at your phone, or picturing the inside of your refrigerator trying to decide what to reheat for dinner tonight.

You've got a 30-second window to process the fact that your kid is on the ground and not getting up. This half-minute will feel more like half an hour as you catastrophize about how this incident will change

not just your plans to pick up toilet paper on the way home, but the rest of your life. Oh, and you're holding your breath the whole time. While you're busy predicting this bleak future, the referee is deciding whether to wave the coach onto the field and the coach is deciding whether he wants to go. Since neither has any medical training, these two decisions are based entirely on a telepathic game of rock, paper, scissors. When the coach's rock is covered by the ref's paper, you'll see the official tap his watch and motion to the coach, who will then attend to your child with all the medical training of a five-year-old with a Fisher-Price doctor kit.

Maybe you can't be with your kid right now, but you are not alone. The moms will lean in close, craning their necks to show you they are with you in this moment. Also, remember, your kid's injury means their kids get more playing time. Now, if you've got a son out there, keep an eye on the dads. They will likely peel off. If they gravitate away from the field, heads down, shuffling their feet, you have your first clue as to the nature of your kid's injury. Because with the exception of keeping each other posted on the score of the much-more-important college football game they are following on their phones, or ganging up on the referee to tell him he's *Fucking blind and has shit for brains because he just let some asshole kid get away with murder*, these men rarely acknowledge each other. So when they walk away from the sideline and form a loose cluster, hands deep in their pockets, not making eye contact, you know. They will feign concern, exude pride, and quietly crack jokes about how it feels to take a hit to the beans.

How to Survive Your Kid's Game-Time Injuries

Nothing prepares you for watching your kid get hurt playing soccer. You may handle couch-hopping contusions, bookshelf-scaling scratches, and backyard body damage with the tranquility of a Buddhist monk. And maybe cleaning cuts, administering albuterol, and even zipping over to urgent care induces less anxiety than remembering at midnight that you haven't packed lunch for the next day's field trip. But once your kid starts playing soccer (read: putting their body in physically dangerous situations), you'll realize that all that early accident experience didn't add up to much, especially from the emotional altitude of the sideline. But with proper training, you can adapt.

1. Practice Doing Nothing

The soccer field is No Man's Land for parents. If something is really wrong—like ambulance-wrong—you'll be waved on. Otherwise, don't even think about crossing the white line of demarcation. Make no mistake. It will be hard—like not-glancing-at-your-kid's-phone-screen hard. Every muscle in your body will try to pull you out of your seat. Don't go. Start building resistance at home: ignore the peanut butter knife on the edge of the sink. Step over the balled-up sock on the stairs. Pretend you don't see the light that's on in an empty room.

Injuries   119

2. Trust the Unprofessionals

The referee is either retired from accounting, works in IT, or is 12 years old. He is also your child's first responder. He decides if your kid's injury is even worth stopping the game for. If it is, your coach, who works in finance, will slow jog (read: walk normally just with his elbows bent) to where your kid is crumpled in the grass. The other players then join him, and soon your child will be completely blocked from view, surrounded by people who may not know the first thing about first-aid protocols.

3. Get Ready to Be Famous

The moment the game is paused, all the parents will either start staring at you, talking to you, or scribbling in their gratitude journal because they are not you. Probably all three. Think of it like it's the Oscars, and you're the shoo-in nominee who didn't win. Eyes will be on your reaction. Be prepared. Think about using your camera's selfie mode to practice looks like, it's-just-my-allergies, I'm-sure-the-bruise-will-fade-before-picture-day, and I-swear-I-saw-an-urgent-care-around-the-corner.

4. Find Some Inner Peace

People around you will be as unhelpful as possible. They'll mean well. Probably. Most of them. It just might not seem like it based on the words coming out of their mouths. As you search for a glimpse of your child across the field, the diagnosing begins. The other parents will proclaim that your kid has an ankle sprain, groin pull, ACL tear, muscle cramp, strained hammy, or concussion. Followed by a story about their friend's coworker's kid who had the exact same thing and [insert the most traumatic outcome you can think of here].

SURVIVING SOCCER

5. Choose Your Own Ending

The first few seconds after your kid gets hurt are critical because that is when you'll decide the seriousness of the injury. You'll do it with a calculation that includes but is not limited to the game's score, its importance to the season, your horoscope, and the likelihood that you left your garage door open. Do the math carefully, then decide whether to yell, *"Get up you're fine!"* or start posting all your kid's sports equipment on eBay.

This forced shift from being hands-on when your kid gets hurt to, basically, eyes-on, is a big one, but you've handled worse. Just stay planted in your seat and practice your who-me?-I'm-not-nervous face.

Hot Tip: A Case for the Year-Round Arm Cast

Remember wanting to wrap your kid in bubble wrap when they were learning to walk, climb trees, or rappel from the loft in your living room? You were 100 percent onto something. Now that they're a soccer player, all they need is an arm cast. According to the rules of most soccer clubs, if their arm is in a cast, you *have* to wrap it. So, practically speaking, you're just one family craft night away from turning your dream into a springy, cushiony reality.

Follow these simple steps and you'll have one less limb to worry about—maybe even two:

1. Identify your child's dominant arm, the one they go in hard with in a challenge. If you're not sure which arm, or you want extra protection, go ahead and cast both arms.
2. Remember, no ref is going to ask you if your kid's arm is *really* broken. (If they do, just yell that that's a HIPAA violation.)

3. Watch a few of the 169,000 videos on YouTube about how to make an arm cast. Note that plaster takes a good 24 hours to set, so allow enough time before the next game.
4. Have fun with it. Let your kid pick their favorite color.
5. Once the creative juices are flowing, work on the back story, uh, break story, together. Encourage them to think big, like base-jumping, volcano-boarding, barrel-over-Niagara-Falls big.
6. Add authenticity by inviting their friends to sign the cast. And if they don't have any friends, they will now—everyone knows kids think casts are cool.
7. Double-check your club's rules. Most say casts need to be bubble-wrapped, but some require foam padding, and, honestly, that's even better.
8. Wrap your kid's casted arm(s) and send them into the game knowing you've given them a springy bumper for on-field collisions, and provided reinforcement for their growing bones.

Once you've casted, there's no going back. Feel free to leave the cast(s) on for the duration of the season. You may want to take little breaks (sorry) between seasons, but keep your supplies handy (and maybe pick a new color!) for when practices start up again. And sure, they may complain that the cast is "itchy," "sweaty," or "uncomfortable," but so is menopause, and women put up with that for years.

SURVIVING SOCCER

First-Aid Field Test
Assess Your Skills

Situation 1: Your kid cramps up in the middle of a game.
- A. Grab your emergency bottle of pickle juice.
- B. Dig through the center console of your car for mustard packets.
- C. Yell across the field that they're fine and should stop complaining.
- D. Tell them if they had eaten the banana you gave them earlier they wouldn't be cramping now, would they?

Situation 2: Your kid takes a ball to the face, resulting in a bloody nose.
- A. Put Jell-O powder on their tongue so they can stick it to the roof of their mouth and let the gelatin clot the blood.
- B. Stuff a tampon up their nose.
- C. Yell across the field that they're fine and they should be happy because they finally look like they're trying.
- D. Tell them they better not get any blood in your car.

Situation 3: Your kid is bleeding, this time from an arm or leg.
- A. Pull super glue out of your first-aid kit.
- B. Pull a bandage out of your first-aid kit.
- C. Yell across the field that they're not bleeding that bad.
- D. Tell them they really better not get any blood in your car.

Injuries

Situation 4: Your kid says it's too painful to run because their skin chafes.
   A. Dig your travel deodorant out of the center console so they can rub it along their legs.
   B. Scour the sideline for a diaper bag and fish out petroleum jelly.
   C. Yell across the field that you don't see anyone else having (air quotes) "chafing issues" and they should just play through it.
   D. Tell them if they'd moved their uniform from the washer to the dryer when you reminded them to, they wouldn't be playing in damp shorts and having this problem, would they?

Situation 5: Your kid got stung by one of the bees that hangs out on the Gatorade bottles.
   A. Pull hemorrhoid cream out of your first aid kit, coat the sting area to quickly reduce inflammation and pain.
   B. Flag down the Kona Ice truck, explain that you just need ice, and no, you do not want Strawberry'd Treasure syrup or Cryin' Key Lime, just the shaved ice, please, and no, not the Orange Ya' Happy either, just some fluffy ice in a cup, that is all.
   C. Yell across the field that if they were actually playing and not sitting on the bench, this wouldn't have happened.
   D. Tell them the bee is probably dead now, so who really has it worse?

Interpret Your Score
   Mostly As—You're a medical MacGyver.
   Mostly Bs—You can keep your kid in the game, but it ain't pretty.
   Mostly Cs—You played football back in the day, so you know *real* injuries.
   Mostly Ds—Hello, Nurse Ratched.

SURVIVING SOCCER

Fine-Tune Your Urgent Care-Dar

Most game-time injuries can be soothed with one or more of the following: ice, rest, electrolytes, ice, empathy, praise, ice, kettle corn, or a reminder that the game is almost over and you're picking up pizza on the way home. Nevertheless, on a handful of occasions, "picking up pizza" will turn into "running by urgent care."

You already have a favorite urgent care near your home, the trampoline park, and each of the grandparents' houses. Maybe you have your own parking space. Possibly an engraved plaque in one of the exam rooms. This level of experience may take the sting out of everyday mini-emergencies, but what about when your kid gets hurt at a game that's out of town? Where will you go? You don't want to be stanching blood with one hand and Googling with the other.

In the vein of keeping backup shin guards on your person at all times, you need a backup plan in case whatever game-time injury your kid sustains can't be fixed with something you have in your car.

When Waze gives you the five-miles-to-your-exit warning, it's time to start making your plan. From here to the field, any option you spot is geographically viable. While the left side of your brain is following directions, the right side is now on sign patrol. Pay close attention. Some clinics will be well-marked and clearly visible from the street, while others will be tucked away inside a Food 4 Less.

You know your crew better than anyone, so if you're a straight-to-the-hospital family, then own it. Suburban soccer meccas may be a cornucopia of medical treatment options, but there's no use messing around with a doc-in-a-box, when only a level-1 trauma center will ease your worried mind. Train your eyes on those little blue "H" signs.

The moment you see the hospital campus, drop a pin. Then, quickly, before you pass it, do a comprehensive visual scan. This could be tricky

Injuries   125

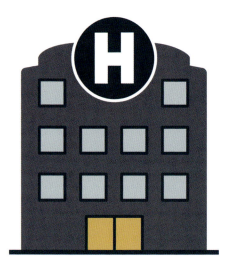

since you're also listening to your phone for directions, watching the road, and regretting how much coffee you drank during the drive. Scope out the parking situation. You need specifics. Can you enter the lot directly from the main road or a side street? How much does parking cost? Can you pay with a card or is it cash only? Do you see a sign with a QR code? Do you know how to use a QR code? How full is the lot? How far away is the entrance to the ER? Do you consider your kid carryable at that distance?

If you're not a hospital-first family, still note them as you pass, of course, because you never know, but good old-fashioned urgent care is the gold standard of reliability. You can always count on a long wait, a steep bill, and your kid getting his very own sling, brace, or crutch—and a much lower chance of vying for the doc's time with car-accident and gun-shot victims.

Your spotting abilities may be a little rusty. Back at home, your favorite urgent cares are programmed into your brain like speed dial. You may not consciously even see them anymore. One moment you're hearing *that* cry, or seeing *that much* blood come out of your kid, and the next thing you know you're using martial arts moves you don't even know you have to kick the automatic door button so you can carry, push, or drag your kid inside.

When you're in a city you don't know, you need to really think about what to look for. Fortunately for you, urgent care marketing teams don't strive for Super Bowl commercial–level creativity. If a sign has red letters, is in all caps, and is wedged into a strip mall or outparcel, it's either going to be urgent care or fast food.

Also, don't overlook the less obvious locations. Plenty of medical clinics are tucked inside groceries, drug stores, and wholesale clubs, which means easy parking, plus snacks and cheap entertainment while you wait.

While you're scanning both sides of the road, trying to decide if the speed limit is 25 or 50, and thinking about how you still have to pee really badly, don't worry about writing down each one you see. Just clock their approximate location with a detail you'll remember, like: it's between a shooting range and a Chuck E. Cheese; it's in front of a kitty cafe, which reminds you that cats sure are easier than kids; or it's in a center with a used record store that might just have that R.E.M album you've been looking for.

By now you're close enough to the field that you need to wake up your kid. And, lucky for you, kids make wonderful spotters. Enlist their help. Pretend it's a game of I Spy or just offer them a dollar for each clinic they spot. (It's a lot cheaper than the tenner Kai's dad gives him for every goal he scores and immensely more practical.)

By the time you get to the field, you should have five to 10 options. Once you deposit your kid with their team and they're immersed in the pregame warm-up, it's time to narrow your list. Start with the easy cuts.

For example, cross off the urgent care that's across the street from the field. On a tournament weekend, it will be packed, and by the time your kid's sprained ankle is diagnosed, the crutches will all be gone.

Now start sleuthing online. Which locations offer on-site X-rays? What does Google say about their busiest time of day? Do they take online appointments, and if so, are there any available right after your game ends? Cross-check their Google, Yelp, and Solv reviews. If any doctors are listed, dig at least 10 pages into their search results.

Once you knock a few off the list or, even better, prioritize a couple, it's time to crowdsource some feedback from people you trust. Go ahead and make a post on your Facebook page or in any private Soccer Parent groups you belong to. Tell them which ones you're considering and ask if anyone has anything to add.

Once you're down to one really solid option, type the address into your navigation app and go enjoy what's left of your kid's game.

CHAPTER 10

Cheering

Ninety percent of parenting is just using the right verb at the right time.

If You're Not Screaming, You Must Not Care

More often than not, your team's admin will be the nicest parent on your team. Generous with their time, patient with all the follow-up emails you send asking if they got your first email, and the one person you can sit or stand next to when you feel totally out of place. Consider the admin like the dog who is happy to let you hang out with him at a party where you don't know anyone. Just don't forget that your admin will always have an ulterior motive—keeping all the parents from provoking one of the coach's make-the-kids-run-until-they-puke moods.

Your admin is no dummy. Those giant lollipops she handed out at kickoff? Not a kindness. Not a treat. Not a thank-you for finally turning in that form she's been asking you to sign and return for four weeks. It's a strategy. The longer your mouth is occupied with a sugary treat, the less time you have to coach, complain, or coddle from the sidelines.

But if you're going to cheer your child in a manner that tells everyone that you care—and know—more than anyone else, then you've got more than hard candy to contend with. The competition is stiff.

Do not assume that, with all the food, shelter, overpriced brand-name clothing, Wi-Fi, video games, streaming services, snacks, and vacations you have provided your child during their lifetime, that their attention and allegiance will be yours, because you will be wrong.

First of all, there's your kid's coach on the opposite side of the field giving out one set of directions. Whether he's a screamer, a low-talker, or one of those coaches who communicates purely with nonverbal expressions of disappointment, you can bet he's told every child on that field what to do and when and how to do it. Your kid will only follow his instructions 50 percent of the time, but that means they will follow this man's instructions 50 percent of the time.

The coach isn't the only distraction out there. Any time your kid has the ball or is about to get the ball, every other child on the team will be screaming their name the way you do after the 19th time you've had to yell up the stairs to tell them to get their dirty socks off the kitchen table so everyone can finally eat dinner.

Then there's the referee. During the day the ref either works as some company's IT guy or is a substitute history teacher, but for 60 minutes he has all the power in your world. He will expect that he has

SURVIVING SOCCER

your child's full attention whenever he wants it. He will tell him where not to stand, how not to stand, where not to throw the ball in, how not to throw the ball in, what not to say, how not to move, and where not to put his foot, hand, or elbow. And what he has to say counts twice as much as what anyone else in the vicinity of that field can utter. Plus, he's got a whistle.

Lastly, your biggest competition, the other spectators. You will share every one of your child's soccer games with a few dozen time-starved, traffic-weary, sunburned/freezing/rain-drenched/bug-bitten, highly competitive parents who are only aware of half the rules of soccer and understand even fewer of them. They love their kid as much as you love yours, and probably quite a bit more. This is the baggage behind every cheer, declaration, and ultimatum they make, but it's only half as important as what's underneath it, a mountain of issues they really should be sharing with a therapist.

You've seen the behavior that fans are capable of in professional sports. Now multiply that passion by I-gave-birth-to-you pride and divide it by don't-embarrass-me distress.

That's what you've got to contend with as you innocently try to cheer your kid on from the sideline. But don't worry, I've got the tips you need to make the impression you're after.

One of your best tools is volume. Don't be fooled into thinking loudest is best. Depending on your specific situation, dial it up or down for a strategic advantage.

Cheering 131

Ideal Volume Levels for Sarcasm, Contempt, and More

VOLUME LEVEL:
Under your breath.
TONE: Typically sarcastic, but can run the gamut from relief to contempt.
TARGET: Intended to be discreetly overheard by one to two people, max, for their entertainment but with no intention of acknowledgment or social interaction.

VOLUME LEVEL:
Your indoor voice.
TONE: Mild-mannered, but with the confidence that others definitely will want to hear what you have to say.
TARGET: Shared for the benefit of nearby friends and acquaintances who believe you to be an entertaining authority on the game.

WELCOME TO THE HYPOCRISY, LEAVE YOUR INHIBITIONS IN THE CAR

- Don't feel the least bit hypocritical criticizing your child, loudly, in front of everyone, for not being able to do something you couldn't have done when you were in the best shape of your life.
- If you're okay with giving your kid an allowance for taking out the trash, then you've got no business wincing when someone offers their kid a $20 each time he scores.
- When all else fails, consider repetition. "Shoot! Shoot!! SHOOT!!!"
- A complete understanding of the rules is by no means a prerequisite for accusing someone of breaking them. "That was so offsides [sic]!"

SURVIVING SOCCER

VOLUME LEVEL: Your outdoor voice.

TONE: Animated, but not always in a bad way.

TARGET: A passionate declaration broadcast to everyone in attendance, underscoring how committed you are to your feelings about a particular play.

VOLUME LEVEL: Your I-can't-even voice.

TONE: Simply articulated exasperation.

TARGET: A carefully chosen word or phrase that drips with an emotion you don't feel comfortable sharing with the relevant person at the relevant time, instead projecting it to a player, official, or spectator in your vicinity.

- Go ahead and tell your kid he's not running fast enough, even at the end of a game. But you may want to catch your breath from standing up out of your chair first.

- Don't let your questionable 20/40 vision keep you from insisting that you know better than anyone else who was in the immediate proximity of the play, that the ball never touched your kid's hand.

- It doesn't matter that you've never actually played soccer before. If you believe that somebody else's kid should have passed to your kid instead of taking the shot themselves, then go ahead and tell them they don't know what they're doing.

Cheering

The War Against (Certain) Words

I'm here to guide you away from dangerous grammatical territory: verbs. Back in school, you didn't hate grammar for nothing. Now it's come back to exact its revenge.

Here's the thing. When you're watching your kid play soccer, just about everything that will naturally sneak from your brain to your mouth will be 1) a verb, and 2) off the table. At no point during a game (or before a game or after a game) should you tell your child what they should do on the soccer field or, more importantly, what they should have done five or more seconds ago on the soccer field.

The secret I'm going to tell you is this: they know. They do. They are well aware—possibly even more than you—that, had they run faster/tried harder/turned around sooner/pulled up their socks/worn their retainer/practiced their clarinet/eaten the banana you handed them in the car, they would have gotten to the ball first, and the other team wouldn't have scored. They know.

So, no verbs. None.

Now, you're probably thinking, *This is easy. Piece of cake. Kid's stuff.* And, my personal favorite, *I would never.* No, you wouldn't. Neither would I. Neither would any parent worth the weight of the heavy gilded frame in which their parenting diploma is displayed...oh, right.

Regardless. You wouldn't. Not on *this* page. Not when we're sitting here like adults.

But you will. You do. We all do. Like it or not, we're all next-page parents. Because we care. Too much. Right?

All I can really do is tell you to bookmark the next page. Share it with your child's current/future therapist, someday spouse, or just save it for when your adult-child starts wondering out loud why their boss criticizes them for lacking confidence in their work.

 SURVIVING SOCCER

Go! Run! Tuck in your shirt! Now!

Sit! Kick! Who was that to?! Keep it up there!

Time!

Talk! Look! Keep playing! Where were you?!

Look!

Pass! Move! What are you doing?!

Lock it in!

Shoot! Sprint! Pay attention!

Hurry! Hustle! Why am I paying for you to stand there?! Stop playing with your hair!

Win it! Go to! Are you even paying attention?! Why did you do that?!

Boot it! Get up! What were you thinking?!

Clear it! Jump in! She's coming! Two minutes left!

Shoot it! Look up! This is important! The game is almost over!

No, turn! Be strong! This is your last chance! Your shorts are on backward!

Stay on it! Try harder! Stop ball-watching!

Run faster! Play smarter! C'mon! Talk to each other!

Shoot now! See who's open! One on! Two on! Get your head in the game!

Keep playing! Do something! Play to the whistle! Stop letting your team down!

Pay attention! Beat him! Come on, Fumble Feet!

Lock it in! Get open! Stop watching!

Be there! Stop the ball! Run faster or no video games later! That's your ball!

Make a run! Get up there! Don't just stand there!

Get in there! Get back! Start playing or you're walking home!

Get onsides! Get back now!

As mentioned, volume is a key variable, but your voice is not the only tool at your disposal. If you want to up the impact, a cow bell, air horn, tambourine, or trumpet are some of your most packable options, but don't underestimate the power of a righteous clap.

Righteous Clapping—Timing Is Everything

Of course you'll clap when your kid does something great, but that's just the beginning. Did you know there was volume control on clapping? Louder, more singular claps or shorter, fevered applause comes in especially handy when:

- The referee calls a foul on the other team.
- A player on the other team is given a yellow card.
- A player on the other team is given a red card.
- Your spouse suggests picking up dinner on the way home instead of cooking.
- Your team scores a goal after the other team commits a foul.
- Your team scores a goal to even up the score.
- Your team scores a goal to take the lead.
- Someone in the crowd announces the score of the college football game you'd rather be watching.
- The other team's coach is issued a warning.
- The other team's coach is ejected from the game.
- The other team's coach is carried away in a stretcher.

2–4–6–8, Who Do Fans Love to Hate?

Welcome to high school soccer. Don't worry if you're not there yet; these traditions aren't going anywhere. They're as deeply rooted in our culture as painting the senior rock and drawing penises on bathroom stalls.

You thought you finally got a handle on the whole cheering system, but I'm here to tell you, there's more to learn. Introducing: rivalries. The good news is, you've got your whole student body on your side. The bad news is, your opponents do too.

Now, you may hear that high school soccer is different from club because it's more physical or not as stylish as what you're used to watching. But the real difference isn't on the turf, it's in the bleachers.

Thanks to the creativity and resourcefulness of teenagers, their cheers take on a particular bite. One that's oddly specific and personal.

Things the other school's fans makes fun of:

- Your team's record
- Your football team's record
- Your school's GPA
- Your mother
- Your mother's GPA
- Your name
- The way you spell your name
- The ball you missed
- The ball you shot too high
- The ball you shot too wide
- The ball that hit you in the face
- Your hair
- Your height

Cheering 137

- Your cleats
- Your ZIP code
- Your coffee order
- Your keeper
- Your backup keeper
- Your backup keeper's mother

CHAPTER 11

It All Started So Innocently

You signed your kid up for soccer because it was something to do. And football looked dangerous. Baseball/softball games last forever. You already predicted your kid wasn't coordinated enough for dance (and you were right). And who needs lacrosse when kids are already so good at beating each other with sticks?

Soccer is straightforward. Kick the ball into the other team's goal. Keep the ball out of your goal. Don't use your hands.

You never thought it would stick. You'd keep your kid active for a few months and expose them to some new lessons and people. They'd get a colorful jersey with their name on it that they'd insist on wearing every single day. And that would be it.

Then, out of nowhere, you're a Soccer Parent. Suddenly you're leaving work early, showing up to family gatherings late, and answering invitations for lunch, a show, a wedding, or a court summons with, "I can't, my kid has practice," or, "Sorry, it's a tournament weekend."

You spend years telling everyone who asks about the insane amount of time soccer siphons from your life that you love how it teaches your kid life lessons. You drone on about the value of being on a team. You regurgitate the benefits of exercise as you casually drop childhood obesity statistics and sermonize about the dangers of screentime. You tearfully describe the coping skills you wish you'd learned at their age. And you act like the score doesn't matter because your kid builds character each time they work their hardest, even if they don't succeed.

Yeah, right.

Winning Is Everything

Let's not kid ourselves. We're not here for life lessons. That's what family game night is for.

You put your kid in soccer to win. You fake blubber to your boss about going to yet another funeral so you can leave work in time to get to the field and watch your kid score goals. You spend your weekend driving back and forth across the state to see them pound another team. You suffer through savage wind chills to be there when they ruin another team's winning streak.

You *need* to win. You *need* your team to beat that team. Especially that one with the cowbell mom. But really any team. You need to jump out of your chair and pump your fist. You need to hoot and holler. You need to high-five the person sitting next to you, even if it's that dad who never uses hand sanitizer after the porta john.

Now here's the part no one else will tell you. One of the greatest joys of winning is knowing the other team did not. When you win, you steal something that someone else thought was theirs. Something important: the belief that they're better than you. Now *that* feels amazing. And it's socially acceptable. (Whereas actual theft is not.) We're supposed to win, right? Winning is American.

The truth is, soccer is never just a game because it's not just the kids on the pitch who win. When your kid wins, it rights the wrongs that happened nowhere near the field. That 5–0 pummeling of an old rival is the acceptance you can't seem to get anywhere else. The 3–2, come-from-behind victory is proof that every once in a blue moon life is fair.

So don't be fooled. Winning is everything. Because someone always wins. Someone gets the last piece of pizza. Someone has their idea chosen at work. And someone gets to pass the slow-as-molasses Buick before the freeway narrows to one lane. Why not you?

And that's why we do it. That's why we give up on regular exercise and having a social life. That's why the rush of getting there on time feels better than a full night's sleep. That's why we care more about the comfort of the front seat of our car than the front room of our house. That's why we become experts at back routes to every park in the city and knowing which gas stations will have the most promising dinner options and least offensive bathrooms.

Like the kid who spends all 50 arcade tokens on The Claw because they know if they keep at it they'll eventually snag the sparkly unicorn that's miraculously staying afloat in a sea of high-bounce balls, you keep at it. Sign-ups, tryouts, training, extra training, private training, special training, more training, long drives, late nights, lost weekends,

It All Started So Innocently

and the kind of weather that can bring you to your knees if only you could still feel them.

You keep registering. You keep schlepping. And you keep cheering. Because sitting there on the grassy sideline, in the cool crisp fall air that smells faintly of leaf piles, pumpkin spice lattes, and the porta john behind the field, you know you've got what it takes to survive soccer.

Acknowledgments

It's easy for me to complain about being a Soccer Parent—the thousands of miles I drove to get my kids to the field, the pouring rain/freezing snow/blistering heat I sat through to watch them play, and all the emergency trips to Dick's for forgotten equipment I reminded them three times to bring. But had Noah and Max not fallen in love with this game, I would have missed so much. Thank you to my boys for 16 years of car conversations, stinky postgame hugs, and excuses to leave work early. I loved to watch you play.

I could not have done any of this (gestures broadly) without the love, support, and like-minded sarcasm of my husband and best friend, Mark. Thank you for making Team Scholl the best team I've ever been on.

Thanks to my parents, Dick and Joyce Sabgir, for signing me up for soccer when I started kindergarten, braving the elements to watch me run down the field and kick a ball, and convincing all their soccer-grandparent friends that they need to buy this book.

Thanks to Carl and Nancy Scholl for letting us bring soccer into their world, and for always coming to games with an extra blanket/chair/umbrella, along with a snack bag for whichever grandson wasn't on the field that day.

This book wouldn't exist without the candid feedback and ongoing encouragement of my writing mentor, Sarah Chauncey, who, after reading my 80,000-word, soccer-parent memoir in 2019 asked if I'd consider turning it into a humor book instead.

I owe so, so much to Deb Rycus, who put the spit-shine on this book, section after section, week after week, during a COVID year of Friday morning video calls. She made each page cleaner, smarter, and funnier. She was the editor, friend, and cheerleader I needed, every step of the way.

I would not have gotten through the early years of soccer parenting without the support, laughter, and communal eye rolls of my first soccer-parent friend, Luann Hoover. I was lucky to have her as a sounding board for so many years of "Is it just me?" questions that became the foundation for this book, and even luckier that we became friend-friends along the way.

And I would not have gotten through the later years without my last soccer-parent friend, Stephanie Loucka. I am forever indebted to her for all the times she answered my "Which field are we on?" texts, and even more grateful for the "I just snarfled my water" texts she'd send when I shared new ideas for the book. I'm so glad we graduated to friend-friends.

Thank you to Shawn Wolfe for years of friendship, encouragement through this whole process, and willingness to share not just her soccer-parent perspective, but a glimpse behind the curtain from her years being the coach's wife.

To my talented and similarly soccer-obsessed friend Gabe Shultz, my heartfelt thanks for bringing Carpool Confidential (the precursor to *Surviving Soccer*) to life and creating the design foundation that moved this idea forward. I look forward to hearing his soccer-parent stories for years to come!

Erin Rosenberg and I raised our soccer players in different states and at different times, but I'm grateful for the generosity of her time to read early drafts and share feedback.

So many thanks to Asia Mape for her passion for positive sports parenting. I still remember the first time I stumbled across her site, ILoveToWatchYouPlay.com, and found a kindred spirit. She graciously agreed to post my essays and has been a generous supporter and sharer of my writing, most specifically, helping me find a path to turn my manuscript into something really real.

I was so lucky to find Tim Brandhorst, who changed my world the day he said, "I think you've got something here," guided me into the world of publishing, and believed enough for the both of us that we'd sell this book.

To Joni Cole and the lovely ladies of the secret Thursday Night Group, my deep appreciation for their careful reading, smart feedback, and making me feel like an honorary Vermonter.

Thanks to all my colleagues and clients who swallowed their judgment each time I had to arrange a meeting around my carpool schedule.

And to all the Soccer Parents I did time with on the sidelines or bleachers over the years, thank you for the memories, and no, your kid's warm-up jacket is not in my kid's bag.

About the Author

Karen Scholl has lived every aspect of the soccer-parent experience—from devotion to frenzy, elation to exhaustion. Over 16 years, she froze inside fleece-blanket igloos, rushed to get to fields on time, and waited in sweltering porta john lines—all for the chance to watch her kids chase a ball down the field. One rainy soccer Saturday, weighed down by an over-stuffed carry-all and a broken canvas chair, while desperately looking for field D-17 Blue,  Karen had a revelation: writing about the chaos of raising kids who play soccer was the only way she would survive it. From then on, when she wasn't spectating or driving the equivalent of 3.5 trips around the Earth to shuttle her sons and various carpoolees to more than 2,000 soccer practices, games, tournaments, and tryouts, she started writing it all down.

Karen is also a copywriter and creative director, working for organizations and brands ranging from local start-ups to global enterprises.

Author photograph by Stacie Bowers Photography